TOP 10
SAN FRANCISCO

JEFFREY KENNEDY

EYEWITNESS TRAVEL

Left **San Francisco Museum of Modern Art** Right **Surfers, Pacific Ocean**

LONDON, NEW YORK,
MELBOURNE, MUNICH AND DELHI
www.dk.com

Produced by Sargasso Media Ltd, London

Printed and bound by
South China Printing Co. Ltd., China

First American Edition, 2003
14 15 16 17 10 9 8 7 6 5 4 3 2 1

Published in the United States by DK Publishing,
345 Hudson Street,
New York, New York 10014

**Reprinted with revisions 2004, 2006,
2007, 2008, 2009, 2010, 2011, 2012, 2013, 2014
Copyright 2003, 2014 © Dorling Kindersley
Limited**

Published in the UK by Dorling Kindersley Limited.

A catalog record for this book is available from the
Library of Congress

ISSN 1479-344X
ISBN 978-1-46541-007-8

Within each Top 10 list in this book, no hierarchy
of quality or popularity is implied. All 10 are, in the
editor's opinion, of roughly equal merit.

MIX
Paper from
responsible sources
FSC™ C018179
www.fsc.org

Contents

San Francisco's Top 10

The information in this DK Eyewitness Top 10 Travel Guide is checked regularly.
Every effort has been made to ensure that this book is as up-to-date as possible at the time of
going to press. Some details, however, such as telephone numbers, opening hours, prices,
gallery hanging arrangements and travel information are liable to change. The publishers
cannot accept responsibility for any consequences arising from the use of this book, nor for
any material on third party websites, and cannot guarantee that any website address in this
book will be a suitable source of travel information. We value the views and suggestions of
our readers very highly. Please write to: Publisher, DK Eyewitness Travel Guides,
Dorling Kindersley, 80 Strand, London, WC2R 0RL, UK, or email: travelguides@dk.com.

JACKET: Front – **Alamy Images**: Patrick Batchelder bl; **Getty Images**: Alex Zyuzikov c. Spine – **Dorling
Kindersley**: Neil Lukas b. Back – **Dorling Kindersley**: cra, Neil Lukas cla, Andrew McKinney ca.

Left **View from Nob Hill** Right **Dining out**

Around Town

Streetsmart

Contents

Left **Golden Gate Bridge** Right **Japanese Tea Garden, Golden Gate Park**

Key to abbreviations
Adm *admission charge* **Free** *no admission charge* **Dis. access** *disabled access*

SAN FRANCISCO'S TOP 10

SAN FRANCISCO'S TOP 10

TOP 10 San Francisco's Highlights

San Franciscans will, rather candidly, admit that they are the most fortunate people on earth, the occasional earthquake notwithstanding; and most visitors, after a few days of taking in the sights and sounds of this magnificent city, will agree. Anyone who has been here will likely tell you it's their favorite city. The geographical setting evokes so much emotional drama, the light seems clearer, the colors more vivid, the cultural diversity of the ethnic neighborhoods so captivating and inviting, that it's a place almost everyone can fall in love with at first sight.

Golden Gate Bridge 1

The symbol of the city and of California's place on the Pacific Rim, the Golden Gate Bridge is one of the largest single span bridges in the world, connecting San Francisco to Marin County *(see pp8–9)*.

2 Cable Cars

San Francisco's little troopers have endured technological progress, and are now the only system of the kind in the world that still plays a daily role in urban life *(see pp10–11)*.

3 Fisherman's Wharf

Despite rampant tourism and commercialization, the saltiness and authenticity are still to be found here if you take time to look. The views of the bay are unmatched, and you'll have an opportunity to try great seafood and see barking sea lions *(see pp12–13)*.

Alcatraz 4

Although it was a federal prison for just under 30 years, the myth of "The Rock" continues to capture the imagination of visitors. The magnificent views from the ferry ride over are one of the best parts of a visit. *(see pp14–17)*.

Presidio

Lincoln Park

Sutro Heights Park

GEARY BOULEVARD

Richmond

CALIFORNIA

GEARY BOULEV

FULTON STREET

Golden Gate Park 6

LINCOLN WAY

Sunset District

25TH AVENUE

PARK PRESIDIO BOULEVARD

19TH AVENUE

7TH AVENUE

SUNSET BLVD

GREAT HIGHWAY

miles ┐ 0 ┌ km

Chinatown
The exotic feel of one of the world's largest Chinese communities outside of Asia makes this a magnet for locals and visitors alike *(see pp18–19)*.

Golden Gate Park
The city boasts one of the largest public parks in the world, with natural beauty and fine museums *(see pp20–23)*.

Grace Cathedral
Dominating Nob Hill with its timeless beauty, San Francisco's favorite cathedral offers a host of awe-inspiring and historic treasures, including Italian Renaissance masterpieces and stained-glass windows *(see pp24–5)*.

San Francisco Museum of Modern Art
San Francisco's architectural landmark houses 20th-century masterworks of painting, sculpture, and photography, and the edgiest digital installations, and also hosts a number of temporary exhibitions *(see pp26–9)*.

Mission Dolores
The city's oldest building is also the only intact chapel among the 21 California missions that Father Junipero Serra founded in the late 18th century. Its founding just days before the Declaration of Independence makes San Francisco older than the US *(see pp30–31)*.

The Wine Country
The wines from this region have become so internationally recognized that French, Italian, and Spanish winemakers have all established vineyards here. A day trip or, even better, a longer stay shouldn't be missed *(see pp32–5)*.

TOP 10 Golden Gate Bridge

As with most of the world's wonders, many said that the Golden Gate Bridge could never be built – the span was too wide, the ocean too powerful and deep, and the cost too great. But to many more, the Golden Gate, the name John Fremont gave the splendid strait in 1846 (see p39), demanded the realization of its dream bridge. In 1872, railroad tycoon Charles Crocker first conceived the idea, but it took a visionary engineer, Joseph Strauss, to put forth a realistic proposal in 1921. After 10 years of opposition from all quarters, funding was finally secured from A.P. Giannini, founder of the Bank of America (see p39). The bridge opened in 1937, and has been an emblem of San Francisco and America's icon on the Pacific ever since.

Marin Vista Point

For a uniquely powerful view of the bridge while enjoying a Sunday champagne brunch, opt for one of the many cruises on the Bay, departing from the Embarcadero Pier and Sausalito. Quality purveyors are Hornblower Cruises (415-438-8300, www.hornblower.com), and Call of the Sea/Seaward (415-331-3214, www.callofthesea.org).

- Map C1
- (415) 921-5858
- www.goldengate.org
- Cruises operate Mar–Oct

Top 10 Features

1. Deco Style
2. Maintenance
3. Fort Point Lookout
4. Marin Vista Point
5. Star Turns in Movies
6. Protective Barriers
7. Building the Bridge
8. Bridge Celebrations
9. Hiking and Biking
10. Toll System

Deco Style
The bridge owes its striking style to the consulting architect Irving F. Morrow. He simplified the pedestrian railings to uniform posts placed far enough apart to allow for unobstructed, breathtaking views.

Maintenance
Repairing and painting the bridge *(above)* is an ongoing task. The paint protects it from the high salt content in the air, which corrodes the steel components.

Fort Point Lookout
This National Historic Site *(below)* was completed in 1861. It offers soaring views of the bridge's underside and of the ocean's pounding waters.

 The orange color was actually close to the original primer and it complements the natural setting so well that it was kept.

Marin Vista Point
Crossing from the San Francisco side, pull off just before you reach the end of the bridge and take in the startling panorama from the specially constructed Vista Point and look back at the hills and spires of the city. If there's fog, note how the bridge's tower tops disappear in the mist.

Protective Barriers
The Golden Gate Bridge is the number one spot in the world for suicides. As yet there are no effective preventative barriers but there are bars *(above)* for general safety.

Building the Bridge
Joseph Strauss introduced the use of hard hats, goggles, and safety belts for the first time, as well as a vast safety net under the bridge, which saved 19 workers.

Toll System
Since 1937, cars have paid a toll to cross the bridge. Now, only city-bound traffic is charged, and in 2013, the system went fully electronic to ease congestion from stopping at toll booths *(below)*.

The Statistics
The length of the steel wires used to make the cables of the bridge is enough to circle the earth three times. It is also brilliantly "over-engineered" and is said to be five times stronger than it needs to be to withstand the winds and tides it endures daily. At the time it was built, it was the longest suspension bridge in the world (it still ranks ninth) and took just over four years to build. About 40 million vehicles cross the bridge annually, streaming across six lanes of traffic, along its 1.7-mile (2.7-km) length. The bridge is equipped with two foghorns, each with a different pitch, and 360-degree flashing red beacons. The bridge has been closed due to high winds only three times in its history.

Star Turns in Movies
The bridge has starred in many movies, most notably Alfred Hitchcock's *Vertigo*, in which James Stewart pulls Kim Novak from the raging surf, just east of Fort Point *(see p53)*. In the James Bond movie, *A View To A Kill*, Grace Jones and 007 battle it out, both of them clinging to the bridge's aerial heights.

Bridge Celebrations
The bridge opened on May 28, 1937, with some 200,000 pedestrians. Fifty years later, the ritual was repeated *(above)*. May 27, 2012 marked the 75th anniversary.

Hiking and Biking
No visit to San Francisco would be complete without a walk or bike-ride across at least part of the bridge.

Pedestrians may access the east sidewalk from sunrise to sunset daily. In-line skaters and skateboards are not allowed.

🔟 Cable Cars

It's impossible not to love these sturdy little vestiges of another age, as they valiantly make their merry yet determined way up the city's precipitous hills. Yet these San Francisco icons came perilously close to being completely scrapped in 1947, when a "progressive" mayor announced it was time for buses to take their place. An outraged citizenry, under the leadership of "cable car vigilante" Mrs. Friedell Klussman, eventually prevailed, and the whole system was declared a National Historic Landmark in 1964. In the early 1980s, the tracks, cables, power plant, and cars all underwent a massive $60-million overhaul and retrofit. The present service covers some 10 miles (16 km) and utilizes about 40 cars.

Cable car route

🕐 Rather than wait in the long lines at a cable car terminus, do what the locals do and walk up a stop or two, where you can hop on right away for a $6 fee – then hold on!

The $5 fare is for one ride, one direction only, and there are no transfers. Consider getting a CityPass or a Muni Passport for one day ($14) or longer *(see p134)*.

• Cable Car Museum: 1201 Mason St, at Washington; Map M3; (415) 474-1887
• www.cablecar museum.org
• Open Apr–Sep: 10am–6pm daily; Oct–Mar: 10am–5pm daily
• Free

Top 10 Features

1. Cars
2. Bell
3. Grip Person
4. Conductor
5. Cables
6. Braking
7. Cable Car Museum
8. Riding Styles
9. Turntables
10. Routes

Cars

Cable cars come in two types: one with a turnaround system, one without. All are numbered, have wood and brass fittings in the 19th-century style, and are often painted in differing colors.

Bell

During the course of operation up and down the busy hills, the cable car's bell *(above)* is used by the grip person like a claxon, to warn other vehicles and pedestrians of imminent stops, starts, and turns.

Grip Person

The grip person *(below)* must be quick-thinking, and strong to operate the heavy gripping levers and braking mechanisms. The grip is like a huge pair of pliers that clamps onto the cable to pull the car along.

Every grip person develops their own signature ring on the car's bell, and a ringing contest is held annually in Union Square.

Conductor
The conductor not only collects fares, but also makes sure that everyone travels safely, and that the grip person has room to do his job.

Cables
The underground cables are 1.25 inches (3 cm) in diameter and consist of six steel strands of 19 wires each, wrapped around a rope, which acts as a shock absorber.

Turntables
Part of the fun of cable-car lore is being there to watch when the grip person and conductor turn their car around for the return trip. The best view is at Powell and Market streets *(left)*.

Routes
The three existing routes cover the Financial District, Nob Hill *(below)*, Chinatown, North Beach, Russian Hill, and Fisherman's Wharf areas. As these are always important destinations for visitors – and for many residents, too – most people find that a cable car ride will be practical as well as pleasurable.

Braking
There are three braking mechanisms. Wheel brakes press against the wheels; track brakes press against the tracks when the grip person pulls a lever; while the emergency brake is a steel wedge forced into the rail slot.

Riding Styles
There is a choice of sitting inside a glassed-in compartment, sitting on outside wooden benches, or hanging onto poles and standing on the running board *(above)*. The third gives you the sights, sounds, and smells of San Francisco at their most enticing.

Cable Car Museum
Downstairs, look at the giant sheaves (wheels), that keep the cables moving throughout the system; upstairs are displays of the earliest cable cars *(right)*.

Cable Cars and Streetcars
Wire rope manufacturer Andrew Hallidie's cable car system dates from August 2, 1873, when he tested his prototype based on mining cars. It was an immediate success and spawned imitators in more than a dozen cities worldwide. However, 20 years later, the system was set to be replaced by the electric streetcar. Fortunately, resistance to above-ground wires, corruption in City Hall, and finally the 1906 earthquake sidetracked those plans. The cable car was kept for the steepest lines, while the streetcar took over the longer, flatter routes.

 The cables, which cost at least $20,000 each, must be replaced every two to three months due to the terrific wear and tear.

⁊10 Fisherman's Wharf

A certain aura of authenticity still clings to San Francisco's old wharf area, but you'll have to look closely to find the historic details – mostly, it has been overwhelmed by tourism. Nevertheless, it's fun to get a walkaway crab cocktail and a chunk of sourdough bread, and to sidestep the crowds to check out the few remaining fishing boats that still haul in their daily bounty. And after all, what's so bad about taking home a few San Francisco souvenirs?

Fisherman's Wharf sign

🍽 Try one of the Wharf's oldest institutions, Scoma's (Pier 47 & Alcona Way; 415 771-4383), for seafood.

• Map J3 • Anchorage Shopping Center: 2800 Leavenworth St; (415) 775-6000
• USS Pampanito:; Pier 45, Jefferson St; (415) 775-1943; www.maritime.org; Open 9am–8pm daily (winter: 9am–5:30pm Sun–Thu, 9am–7:30pm Fri–Sat); Adm $6–$12
• Ripley's Believe It Or Not!: 175 Jefferson St; (415) 202 9850; www.ripleysf.com; Open mid-Jun–Labor Day: 9am–11pm Sun–Thu, 9am–midnight Fri–Sat; rest of year: 10am–10pm Sun–Thu, 10am–midnight Fri–Sat; Adm $15.99–$21.99
• Wax Museum: 145 Jefferson St; 1 (800) 439-4305, (415) 202-0402; Open 10am–9pm daily; Adm $8–$16
• Aquarium of the Bay:; Embarcadero; 1-888-SEA-DIVE Open 9am–8pm daily (winter: 10am–6pm Mon–Thu, 10am–7pm Fri–Sun); Adm $10–$18

Top 10 Sights

1. Ghirardelli Square
2. Anchorage Shopping Center
3. The Cannery
4. PIER 39
5. USS *Pampanito*
6. Fisherman's and Seaman's Memorial Chapel
7. Fish Alley
8. Aquarium of the Bay
9. Boudin Bakery
10. Ripley's Believe it or Not! and Wax Museum

⁊1 Ghirardelli Square

The Ghirardelli family ran a chocolate factory here from 1859 to 1962. The site *(below)* is now home to upscale shops and eateries *(see pp96–7)*.

⁊2 Anchorage Shopping Center

In the heart of Fisherman's Wharf, with plenty of stores, restaurants, and entertainment.

⁊3 The Cannery

Built as a warehouse in 1907, a makeover was completed in 1967, and it's now the site of some appealing boutiques, as well as tourist shops.

⁊4 PIER 39

Built over a disused pier, this 1978 commercial venture became an instant success for promoting tourism in the wharf area *(below)*. Two floors of shops and eateries, with a large central promenade complete with an antique Venetian carousel, keep drawing in the crowds.

Don't miss the pod of wild sea lions that lounge around the docks just to the west of PIER 39.

USS Pampanito

This vintage submarine *(above)* sank six enemy ships and damaged four others in World War II. You can tour its interior and get an idea of what life was like for the crew.

Plan of Fisherman's Wharf

Boudin Bakery

This is the home of the famous chain of San Francisco sourdough breadmakers. Stop by to try the distinctive crusty round loaf, best enjoyed warm from the oven with plenty of butter.

Ripley's Believe It Or Not! and Wax Museum

These fun-zone denizens *(below)* – found as "attractions" around the world – are a give-away that these blocks of Jefferson Street are pure tourist trap.

Fisherman's and Seaman's Memorial Chapel

This little wooden chapel was built in 1980 as an interfaith memorial to all those who make and have made their living at sea.

Fish Alley

This alley *(right)* is possibly the last vestige of the authentic, workaday wharf. Here you can see fishing boats come in and watch as the catch of the day is landed and prepared for market.

Aquarium of the Bay

The aquarium's transparent tunnel visually immerses you in the San Francisco Bay marine habitat, where thousands of members of diverse ocean fauna disport themselves before your eyes. Video presentations and marine specialist guides help you understand what you're seeing.

The Port of San Francisco

In 1853 the first wharf was built here, and it quickly became a center for maritime-related enterprise, including shipbuilding, and fresh seafood joints. Italians soon monopolized almost every aspect of the fishing industry – even today, most of the eateries along the Wharf bear Italian names. With technology, however, the Bay was fished-out by the 1950s, and any big-time fishing industry went out of business or moved elsewhere.

TOP 10 Alcatraz

To the inmates who were confined on this island prison, in operation from 1934 to 1963, their punishment was not only captivity but also psychological torture. After all, they were right in the midst of one of America's busiest harbors, with small craft darting to and from San Francisco, Oakland, Berkeley, and Sausalito, and they could probably hear the ceaseless procession of automobiles crossing the bridges and honking their horns. They could certainly see the ocean liners as they glided through the Golden Gate to far away ports – all reminding them that life was near, but freedom very far.

View of Alcatraz Island from San Francisco

Picnicking is allowed on the dock, but you'll have to bring your own food. The visitor center does sell water, however.

The weather is often blustery and cold on the island, and the trails and walkways rough. Wear warm clothes and strong, comfortable shoes.

A cell house audio tour explores the prison and its stories. It is available in eight languages and is included in the price of the ticket, as is the ranger-guided tour.

• Alcatraz Cruises (Hornblower) from Pier 33: (415) 981-7625 (tickets and schedules)
• www.alcatrazcruises.com
• Open daily
• Adm: day tours – $18.25 child 5–11 years, $30 adult, $28.25 senior; night tours – $21.75 child 5–11 years, $37 adult, $34.25 senior; family packages available

Top 10 Features

1. Lighthouse
2. Cell Block
3. Exercise Yard
4. Control Room
5. D Block
6. Mess Hall
7. Chapel
8. Broadway
9. Building 64
10. Warden's House

Lighthouse
Alcatraz Island was the site of the very first lighthouse built on the West Coast in 1854. The original lighthouse was replaced in 1909 to tower above the new cell block.

Cell Blocks
The cell house contains four free-standing cell blocks *(below)*. The complex was built by military prisoners in 1911 and was once the largest reinforced concrete building in the world. In all, there were 390 cells, but the population averaged only about 260 at any one time.

Exercise Yard
With the monotonous gloom of being cut off from life, prisoners whose good behavior qualified them for a turn around the walled-in Exercise Yard *(above)* must have felt very relieved. Here, they could walk, rather than pace in their cells, where they spent between 16 and 23 hours every day.

You cannot visit Alcatraz independently – a tour must be booked with the ferry company.

4 Control Room
From this bunker-like facility, reinforced to withstand siege, the guards controlled the 24-hour electric security system. Next to the Control Room was the visiting area, where thick glass separated prisoners and visitors, and conversations were held over monitored telephones.

5 D Block
Any prisoner who transgressed the strict rules would be sent to D Block *(above)*, where some of the 42 solitary confinement cells were kept in total darkness.

9 Building 64
The theater and orientation center are located in the old barracks building behind the ferry jetty *(below)*. The building also houses a bookstore, exhibits, and a multimedia show providing a historical overview of Alcatraz.

10 Warden's House
Until the house burned down in 1970, the warden's home looked out to freedom. Designed in Mission Revival style, the home had 17 large rooms, and sweeping views of the Golden Gate Bridge and San Francisco lights.

The History of "The Rock"

The name "Alcatraz" derives from the Spanish *alcatraces*, for the birds that Spanish explorer Juan Manuel de Ayala observed here when he sailed into the Bay in 1775. In 1850, a presidential order set aside the island for the US Army to build a citadel, but defense became less of a priority and, in 1909, it became a military prison. In 1933 the Federal Government decided to open a maximum-security penitentiary here. Yet Alcatraz was not the "Devil's Island" that many think it was – the conditions, such as one man per cell, were better than other prisons.

6 Mess Hall
Meals were one of the few things prisoners had to look forward to, and they were generally well-fed, to quell rebellion. Note the sample menu on display at the kitchen entrance.

7 Chapel
On top of the guardhouse, a Mission-style military chapel *(above)* was built during the 1920s. It was used as living quarters and a school, as well as a chapel. During the post-1930s prison phase, the building was used to house prison staff.

8 Broadway
The corridor that separates C and B blocks *(left)* was jokingly nicknamed by prisoners after New York City's glittering thoroughfare, famous for its nightlife. The intersection at the end was named "Times Square."

It is advisable to book early as tickets sell out weeks in advance.

Left **Al Capone** Right **Scene from the film** *Escape from Alcatraz*

🔟 Stories from The Rock

1 Robert "Birdman" Stroud
The most famous inmate was dubbed the "Birdman", despite the fact that he was not permitted to conduct his avian studies during his 17 years here. Due to his violent nature Stroud spent most of those years in solitary.

2 Birdman of Alcatraz
This 1962 movie presented Stroud as a nature-loving ornithologist, bending historical fact to the service of a good story.

3 Al Capone
In 1934 Capone was among the first "official" shipment of prisoners. The infamous gangster was assigned menial jobs and treated like every other inmate.

4 George "Machine Gun" Kelly
Jailed in 1933 for kidnapping, Kelly was given a life sentence, and was sent to Alcatraz for 17 years. He was considered a model prisoner by the officers.

Robert "Birdman" Stroud

5 Alvin "Creepy" Karpis
Karpis robbed his way through the Midwest between 1931 and 1936, and earned himself the title Public Enemy Number One. He was imprisoned on Alcatraz from 1936 to 1962. He committed suicide in 1979.

6 Morton Sobell
Charged with conspiracy to commit treason, Sobell arrived on Alcatraz in 1952 and spent five years as its most famous political prisoner, being a victim of J. Edgar Hoover's witch hunt for Communist subversives. Once freed, Sobell returned to live in San Francisco, for many years.

7 Anglin Brothers
The brothers, John and Clarence, are notable as two of five known inmates to successfully escape from The Rock.

8 Escape from Alcatraz
Starring Clint Eastwood as Frank Morris, who escaped along with the Anglin brothers. Again, this 1979 film is largely Hollywood fiction. However, the depiction of prison life is reportedly accurate.

9 Frank Wathernam
The last prisoner to leave Alcatraz, on March 21, 1963.

10 The Rock
Hollywood has never lost its fascination with Alcatraz, as can be seen in this 1996 action thriller, starring Sean Connery.

Top 10 Escape Attempts

Native American Occupation

In 1969 Richard Oakes and 90 Native Americans landed on Alcatraz, set up camp, and demanded the government sell them the island for $24 worth of beads and red cloth. They claimed that this was the price their people had been paid in exchange for an island similar in size nearly 300 years earlier. The government considered forcibly removing the occupiers, but growing public support for the Indians forced officials to renew negotiations. However, in January 1970, while playing on the rooftop of one of the buildings, Oakes' youngest daughter slipped and fell to her death; distraught, he and his family decided to abandon their claim. Sixty Native Americans remained, but as the stalemate dragged on, the majority slowly began to leave – only 15 chose to stay. In June 1970, fires ravaged the warden's house, the recreation hall, the officers' club, and the lighthouse. Following this devastation, government troops staged a pre-dawn raid. The remaining Indians were arrested and the 19-month Indian occupation came to an end.

Liberation Day
One of the occupying Sioux Indians, Fear Forgets, led defiant Liberation Day celebrations on the island on May 31, 1970.

Teepee set up on Alcatraz during the Native American occupation

natown

densely populated neighborhood, with its bright façades, noisy temples, and ethnic restaurants and shops, is like a city within the city – and a place every visit to San Francisco must include. The atmosphere recalls a typical southern Chinese town, although the architecture, customs, and public celebrations are distinctly American hybrids on a Cantonese theme. Overlook the tourist tackiness, check out some of the side alleys, and give yourself time to take it all in.

Colorful awning, Chinatown shop

⚙ Don't drive into Chinatown: it's very congested, and parking is impossible. Take the cable car – all three lines will get you there *(see p11)*.

◯ One of the most popular Chinese restaurants in town is Yank Sing *(see p91)*.

- Map N4
- Golden Gate Fortune Cookies Company: 56 Ross Alley; Map M4; (415) 781-3956
- Old Chinese Telephone Exchange: East West Bank, 743 Washington St; Map M4
- Tin How Temple: 125 Waverly Place, top floor; Map N4;
- Chinese Six Companies: 843 Stockton St; Map N4
- Chinese Historical Society of America Museum and Learning Center: 965 Clay St; Map N5; (415) 391-1188; www.chsa.org
- Chinese Culture Center: Hilton Hotel 3rd floor, 750 Kearny St; Map M5; (415) 986-1822; www.c-c-c.org

Top 10 Sights

1. Chinatown Gate
2. Portsmouth Square
3. Golden Gate Fortune Cookies Company
4. Old Chinese Telephone Exchange
5. Temples
6. Stockton Street Chinese Markets
7. Chinese Six Companies
8. Chinese Historical Society of America Museum and Learning Center
9. Chinese Culture Center
10. St Mary's Square

Chinatown Gate
A gift from Taiwan in 1970, this triple-pagoda southern entrance to Chinatown *(above)* was inspired by traditional Chinese village gates.

Portsmouth Square
This was San Francisco's original town square – here, on July 9, 1846, the US flag was first raised on the Bay, when the port was seized from Mexico. Locals now use the area for *t'ai chi* and games of *mah-jong*.

Golden Gate Fortune Cookies Company
Fortune cookies were invented in San Francisco. Stop by to watch how the skillful workers *(left)* slip the fortune message in the cookie mixture, then fold it into the traditional shapes.

➤ The finest Chinese antiques shops are found at the Chinatown Gate end of Grant Avenue, just inside the gate.

4 Old Chinese Telephone Exchange
This three-tiered pagoda is now the East West Bank, and is the most distinctive work of architectural chinoiserie in Chinatown. It served as the telephone exchange until the 1950s.

6 Stockton Street Chinese Markets
At these authentic produce markets the real smells, sights, and sounds of Chinatown come into sharp focus (above).

Map of Chinatown

9 Chinese Culture Center
The Chinese Culture Center comprises an art gallery and a small crafts shop, featuring the work of Chinese and Chinese-American artists.

10 St Mary's Square
This square is graced by a stainless-steel and rose-granite statue of Sun Yat-sen (below) by San Francisco sculptor Beniamino Bufano.

5 Temples
There are a number of temples that incorporate Confucian, Taoist, and Buddhist elements. The Tin How Temple (below) was founded in 1852 and dedicated to the Queen of Heaven.

7 Chinese Six Companies
This building's brilliant façade is one of the most ornate in Chinatown. The Six Companies was formed in 1882 to promote Chinese interests within the community.

8 Chinese Historical Society of America Museum and Learning Center
This is the home of the Chinese Historical Society's 15,000-piece collection of artifacts, documents, photographs, and replicas that illustrate and explain the Chinese-American experience.

Gold Rush Cantonese
Chinese immigrants began to arrive with the Gold Rush, to get rich quick and return home heroes. As it happened, things turned politically sour in China at the time, and many Chinese stayed in the new land. Unfortunately, there was a racist backlash against them, resulting in the Chinese Exclusion Act of 1882, and Chinatown became a kind of ghetto, full of opium dens and vice. The Act was repealed in 1943, and things have steadily improved ever since.

The Chinese Culture Center sponsors a lively series of lectures and seminars, as well as walking tours of Chinatown.

⁑10 Golden Gate Park

Golden Gate Park is every San Franciscan's beloved backyard. Any weekend finds hundreds of people coming here to play or just to relax and breathe in the heady air. Almost every conceivable sort of recreational activity is available: hiking, running, cycling, golf, tennis, baseball, soccer, volleyball, fishing, and more. There's also the very first children's playground in the US, with the magnificent Herschel-Spillman Carousel, built in 1912 (see p59). Even on a rainy day, the park offers world-class activities in the form of the California Academy of Sciences Natural History Museum, Morrison Planetarium, and, perhaps best of all, the marvelous Steinhart Aquarium (see pp22–3).

Shakespeare Garden entrance

🛈 For information and a map of the park, stop at the McLaren Lodge Visitor Center, originally the home of the park's chief gardener (501 Stanyan St, open 8:30am–5pm Mon–Fri).

• Entrances on Fulton St, Lincoln Way, Stanyan St & the Great Hwy
• Map D4 • (415) 831-2700 • www.parks.sfgov.org • Open sunrise–sunset • Free
• Japanese Tea Garden: Hagiwara Tea Garden Drive; (415) 752-1171; Open 9am–6pm; Adm $7 adult, $5 youth, $3 child/senior
• Strybing Arboretum & Botanical Gardens: 9th Ave; Open Apr–Oct: 9am–6pm; Nov–Mar: 10am–5pm; Free
• California Academy of Sciences: Music Concourse; (415) 379-8000; www.calacademy.org; Open 9:30am–5pm Mon–Sat, 11am–5pm Sun; Adm $20–$30

Top 10 Sights

1 Stow Lake and Strawberry Hill
2 Victorian Conservatory of Flowers
3 Giant Tree Fern Grove and John McLaren Rhododendron Dell
4 Music Concourse
5 Japanese Tea Garden
6 Shakespeare Garden
7 Strybing Arboretum and Botanical Gardens
8 de Young Museum
9 Buffalo Paddock
10 Dutch Windmill and Queen Wilhelmina Tulip Garden

Stow Lake and Strawberry Hill

Strawberry Hill is the island in the middle of this lake. Don't miss the Chinese moon-viewing pavilion on the island's eastern shore.

Victorian Conservatory of Flowers

The park's oldest building, a copy of London's Kew Gardens *(below)*, shelters more than 20,000 rare and exotic plants.

Giant Tree Fern Grove and John McLaren Rhododendron Dell

Coming upon the Giant Tree Fern Grove, with its huge, curling proto-flora gathered around a small central lagoon, is like venturing into a primeval forest. Just a bit farther to the west, the Rhododendron Dell contains the largest array of these gorgeous blooms (850 varieties) of any US garden.

For more parks and gardens **See pp48–9**

FULTON STREET

10 **9**

KENNEDY DRIVE

JF KENNEDY DRIVE

2

CROSS OVER DRIVE

Golden Gate Park

5 **4** **8** **3**

6

1

MARTIN LUTHER KING JR DRIVE

JF

MARTIN LUTHER KING JR. DRIVE

LINCOLN WAY

7

STANYAN STREET

GREAT HIGHWAY

Map of Golden Gate Park

Music Concourse
This area provides the cultural focus for the park, dating from 1894. There are free concerts on Sundays and events sponsored by the San Francisco Opera *(see p56)*.

Japanese Tea Garden
This eternally delightful garden is full of refined detail: bonsai trees, rock gardens, exotic plantings, and pagodas *(above)*.

Shakespeare Garden
This charming English garden features the 200-odd flowers, herbs, and such, mentioned in the Bard's works. Bronze plaques quote appropriate passages.

Strybing Arboretum and Botanical Gardens
This vast area is home to more than 7,000 species from countries with climates similar to that of San Francisco. Environments include a Redwood Nature Trail, a Primitive Plant Garden, and a Biblical Garden.

de Young Museum
Set in a beautiful garden located in the heart of the park, this landmark museum exhibits art from Africa, the Americas, and the Pacific. Also has an astounding collection of textiles, photographs, and modern art *(see p40)*.

Buffalo Paddock
American buffalo were first brought here in 1894. In 1984 a small herd was given a home again, roaming under the eucalyptus trees *(left)*.

Dutch Windmill and Queen Wilhelmina Tulip Garden
The windmill *(above)*, and the tulip garden that surrounds it, were both gifts from the queen of the Netherlands in 1902. The windmill is one of the world's largest and was restored in 1981.

A Miracle of Land Reclamation

The park's more than 1,000 acres are some 3 miles (5 km) long and half a mile (1 km) wide, making it the largest cultivated urban park in the US. There are 27 miles (43 km) of footpaths, winding through gardens, lakes, waterfalls, and forests. But it was not always so. Before the 1870s the entire area was sandy wastes and scrubland. William Hammond Hall made great progress over two decades, then hired Scottish gardener John McLaren in 1890. "Uncle John," as he was known, made the park his life's work, devoting himself to its perfection until his death in 1943, at the age of 97.

The Garden of Fragrance in the Strybing Arboretum is specially designed for the visually impaired to enjoy.

Left **A spiky specimen from the Academy** Right **Clownfish in the Coral Reef exhibit**

Top 10 California Academy of Sciences

1 Swamp
Part of the Steinhart Aquarium, which now holds about 38,000 animals from around the world, the Swamp is home to Claude, the famous albino alligator, alligator snapping turtles, and exhibits on frogs, rattlesnakes, and salamanders.

2 Discovery Tidepool
Stroke a starfish, get cozy with hermit crabs, or pick up a sea slug in this hands-on, hands-wet attraction, part of the California Coast exhibits. Here, you don't have to worry about slippery rocks to get close to these coastal creatures. The pool is staffed by volunteers who will tell you what you're handling and keep the animals safe, too.

3 Coral Reef
This is one of the deepest living coral reef displays in the world, exhibiting a range of aquatic life from the coral reefs and mangroves of the Philippines. Sharks and rays can be seen from the surface, and the coral and reef fish can be viewed close up through underwater windows.

4 The Water Planet
Dozens of tanks and a range of interactive media are used to inform all ages of what it takes to survive under water. A variety of fish, reptiles, amphibians and insects are on display.

5 Rainforests of the World
Visitors can experience four diverse rainforest environments in an enormous glass dome: the Amazonian Flooded Forest, the Borneo Forest Floor, the Madagascar Rainforest Understory, and the Costa Rica Rainforest Canopy. This includes hundreds of tropical plants and a diverse range of creatures: piranhas, flying lizards, poison-dart frogs, parrots, chameleons, and butterflies.

6 California Coast
Explore habitats from salt marshes to turbulent rocky inlets and meet a variety of native fish and invertebrates. The main tank – an exhibit featuring the marine habitats of the Gulf of the Farollones National Marine Sanctuary – is 100,000 gallons in capacity, with large viewing windows, and a crashing wave surge system.

Discovery Tidepool

The Academy has a sustainable facility in Golden Gate Park. For details: www.calacademy.org

7 African Hall

Magnificent dioramas show a range of African fauna, such as the straight-horned oryx, gorillas, and cheetahs, in their natural surroundings, while the human evolution exhibit tracks our species' fascinating history. A colony of African penguins ends the exhibit, viewed through a vast window.

8 Penguin Feeding Time

The colony of black-footed penguins located in African Hall are fed twice daily, and it's always a spectacle that the whole family enjoys. Penguins may waddle on land, but their grace is evident when you observe them dive and glide effortlessly through the water to catch their meal.

9 Morrison Planetarium

Fly through space and time to the very limits of the known universe, and gain a new perspective on the planet we call home, with high-tech exhibits and technology, including an all-digital dome. Shows are presented daily.

State-of-the-art Morrison Planetarium

10 The Living Roof

The museum is topped with a 2.5-acre (1-ha) living roof, planted with over 1.7 million native Californian plants. Take an elevator up to the rooftop deck to enjoy the views and learn about the benefits of sustainable architecture.

Penguin Feeding Time

 Kids love the Naturalist Center, where there are multimedia displays and activities like scavenger hunts.

📖10 Grace Cathedral

The third largest Episcopal cathedral in the US stands on the site of Charles Crocker's Nob Hill mansions, which were destroyed in the 1906 earthquake. Work began on Grace Cathedral in 1910 but it was not finally completed until 1964. It is constructed of steel and concrete, despite its Gothic look, so as to withstand the city's seismic vagaries. The interior is replete with marble and abundant stained glass, and other sumptuous touches both within and without make it one of America's most interesting religious structures.

Façade

⊖ The cathedral has a simple café, located downstairs on the south side of Cathedral Close, along with a shop.

❂ Visit the cathedral during Thursday Evensong (at 5:15pm), when the lighting is at its most dramatic, especially in the summer.

- 1100 California St
- Map N3
- (415) 749-6300
- www.gracecathedral.org
- Open 7:30am–6pm Mon–Fri, 8am–5pm Sat, 8am–7pm Sun

Top 10 Features

1. Carillon Tower
2. East Rose Window
3. Chapel of Grace
4. Doors of Paradise
5. New Testament Window
6. 20th-Century Windows
7. Keith Haring's Altarpiece
8. The Organ
9. Interfaith Labyrinth
10. Labyrinth and Bufano St. Francis of Assisi

Carillon Tower
The belfry contains a carillon of 44 bronze bells, cast in England in 1938. The bourdon bell, which tolls the hour, is the largest carillon bell in the western US. Many of the bells have evocative names, such as Loving Kindness, and Joy to the World.

East Rose Window
This 25-ft (8-m) work of faceted glass *(below)* is the largest in the western US. It symbolizes the themes of the Canticle of the Sun, a devotional poem by St. Francis of Assisi.

Chapel of Grace
This chapel *(above)* was the first completed unit of the cathedral (1930). Its architecture, windows, and apse mural were inspired by the royal Sainte Chapelle in Paris. Its furnishings are a mix of ages and origins, including the medieval French stone altar, the Flemish altarpiece (c.1520), the English Gothic prayer desk, and the painting of the Madonna and Child inspired by Italian Renaissance artist Giovanni Bellini.

The Chapel of Grace seats 120 people and is used for daily services, weddings, and special events.

4 Doors of Paradise

The cathedral doors *(left)* are bronze and gold plate replicas of the ones made for the Baptistry in Florence, Italy. The 10 panels depict Old Testament stories, beginning at the top left with Adam and Eve.

7 Keith Haring's Altarpiece

The AIDS Interfaith Memorial Chapel contains a triptych altarpiece of bronze and white gold *(below)* by the New York artist Keith Haring. It was completed shortly before his own death from AIDS. The central panel shows a multi-armed figure of compassion, while the side panels depict winged souls soaring above.

5 New Testament Window

The theme of this window is brotherhood and the church. Christ stands with a welcoming gesture, with His disciples flanking.

6 20th-Century Windows

The theme of these windows is human endeavor and they depict creative 20th-century Americans, including physicist Albert Einstein, and astronaut John Glenn.

8 The Organ

This monumental organ with 7,286 pipes dates from 1934. Its carved English oak screens show angelic musicians, songbirds, and dragons, as well as the instruments of Christ's Passion in lower portions.

9 Interfaith Labyrinth

The Interfaith Outdoor Labyrinth is a replica of the one at Chartres Cathedral in France. Such labyrinths were used in medieval times to enact the soul's journey through life to salvation; first revived here in a church setting.

Floorplan of Grace Cathedral

10 Labyrinth and Bufano St. Francis of Assisi

Just beyond the entrance is the nave labyrinth, and an appealing statue of St. Francis of Assisi *(above)* by the late San Franciscan sculptor Beniamino Bufano.

Nob Hill

"Nob" was one of the kinder names reserved for the unscrupulous entrepreneurs who built their mansions on this, San Francisco's highest hill *(see p83)*. Some say the name derives from "nabob", the title for a provincial potentate in India; others say it's simply a contraction of "snob", a theory that would also seem plausible. Despite the loss of almost all of the mansions in the 1906 earthquake, the hill's poshness remains, as home to the city's most celebrated luxury hotels.

10 San Francisco Museum of Modern Art

Founded in 1935, the SFMOMA is the only museum in the western US devoted to collecting and exhibiting the full scope of modern and contemporary art. SFMOMA is currently closed while it undergoes a massive building expansion, offering more public areas, expanded educational facilities and flexible gallery space for its growing collection. The new SFMOMA is due to open in 2016. Extensive off-site programming and exhibitions of the collection will be on view at partner museums and be given on loan to museums around the city.

Museum façade

⭐ The museum store will remain open during the renovation, but based in a temporary location.

⭐ Free gallery tours are offered hourly from 11:30am–2:30pm, and at 7:15pm on Thursdays. Meet in the Atrium.

- 151 3rd St
- Map Q5
- (415) 357-4000
- www.sfmoma.org
- Currently closed for major renovations until 2016.
- Museum store: 51, Yerba Buena Lane (between Market and Mission Streets); (415) 357 4035; Open 11am–7pm Mon–Sat, noon–5pm Sun.
- Dis. access
- Adm $18 adult, $12 senior, $11 student with ID, free child 0–12 years; audio tour price varies; free first Tue of month, half-price on Thu evenings

Top 10 Features
1. Exterior
2. Roof Garden
3. 20th-Century European Artists
4. 20th-Century American Artists
5. Bay Area Artists
6. Latin American Artists
7. Photography
8. Electronic & Digital Art
9. Temporary Exhibitions
10. The Catwalk

Key
- First floor
- Second floor
- Third floor
- Fourth floor
- Fifth floor

Exterior
The building was designed by renowned Swiss architect Mario Botta. The 125-ft (38-m) truncated cylindrical turret *(right)* is decorated with Art Deco-style chevrons.

Roof Garden
Featuring a combination of well-known, rarely seen works from the museum's collection, the Roof Garden is not to be missed *(above)*. Sculptures by artists such as Louise Bourgeois, Robert Arneson, and Alexander Calder are on display here.

Entrance

Works from the SFMOMA collection will be on view at various locations around the city and beyond.

3 20th-Century European Artists

These works are located on the second floor. Here you will find important works by Matisse, Miró, Degas, Picasso, Braque, Klee, Mondrian, Duchamp, Dalí, and Magritte, among others.

5 Bay Area Artists

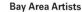

San Francisco Bay Area artists are also represented on the second floor, and include Richard Diebenkorn, Wayne Thiebaud, and Clyfford Still, all with international reputations. Bay Area figurative painters in the collection include Elmer Bishoff, and David Park. Most noteworthy, perhaps, is *California Artist* (1982), a humorous sculptural self-portrait by Robert Arneson in glazed stoneware *(right)*.

6 Latin American Artists

Latin American art is represented most forcefully by the work of muralist Diego Rivera and his wife Frida Kahlo. Other Latin American painters represented include Wilfredo Lam, and Joaquín Torres-Garcia.

9 Temporary Exhibitions

The museum's temporary exhibition spaces may include educational programs, interactive programs, or retrospective exhibitions of the work of contemporary artists such as Yoko Ono and Eva Hess, or the photography of Victorian author Lewis Carroll.

10 The Catwalk

Suspended high up inside the cylindrical turret, visitors can walk the see-through 35-ft (10-m) steel bridge that cuts across the skylight *(left)*, providing dramatic views of the Sculpture Terrace and the Atrium.

7 Photography

One of the museum's strengths; exhibits may include masterpieces by Man Ray, Ansel Adams, and Edward Weston, as well as more avant-garde works.

8 Electronic & Digital Art

Established in 1987, the collection includes multimedia works, moving-image pieces, and video installations by such artists as Brian Eno, Bill Viola, Dara Birnbaum, Matthew Barney, and Nam June Paik.

4 20th-Century American Artists

US artists included here are O'Keeffe, de Kooning, Pollock, Warhol, and Kline. One of the perennial hits of the collection *(above)* is Jeff Koons' iconic ceramic sculpture *Michael Jackson and Bubbles* (1988).

Museum Guide

The museum renovation project will see SFMOMA increase its size to 225,000 ft. This will include a larger gallery space to house their increasing permanent collection of art. The third floor outdoor sculpture terrace will have the biggest public living wall, in the form of a large-scale vertical garden. Live art, film screenings and events will take place on the fourth floor, and a conservation studio will stretch over the seventh and eighth.

Left **Aerial view, the Esplanade** Right **Yerba Buena Center for the Arts Theater**

Yerba Buena Gardens' Features

1 Yerba Buena Center for the Arts Gallery

Changing exhibitions here explore issues of race, class, gender, history, technology, and art.
⊗ 701 Mission St • Map Q5
• (415) 978-2787 • Open noon–8pm Thu–Sat, noon–6pm Sun • Dis. access • Adm
• www.ybca.org

2 Yerba Buena Center for the Arts Theater

Multiculturalism is often the keynote in this 750-seat indoor theater. Performances may range from world-music festivals to Victorian operettas.
⊗ Box Office: (415) 978-2787

3 Moscone Center

Completed in 1981, this building began the renovation of the SoMa district. It was the site of the Democratic Party's convention in 1984. Most of it is underground; above ground the impression is of glass, girders, and gardens. ⊗ Howard St • Map Q5

Map of Yerba Buena Gardens

Moscone Center

4 Esplanade

The Esplanade comprises garden-lined walkways, an inviting lawn, rolling hills, trees, and interesting sculptures. Free weekly concert during the summer festival (www.ybae.org).

5 Rooftop Children's Center and Carousel

Located atop the west wing of the Moscone Center, this complex is all about children. The carousel dates from 1906. There's also an ice-skating rink, a bowling center, a learning garden, and an amphitheater.
⊗ 750 Folsom St • Map Q5

6 Martin Luther King, Jr. Memorial

Featuring words of peace in several languages, this multi-faceted monument incorporates sculpture, a waterfall, and quotations from the Civil Rights leader's speeches and writings.

7 Children's Creativity Museum

This interactive technology and art museum aims to inspire creative impulses in children. There are animation, design, and music studios as well as a wealth of other engaging activities. ⊗ 221 4th St • Map Q5
• (415) 820-3320 • Open 10–4pm Wed–Sun
• Dis. access • Adm • www.creativity.org

8 California Historical Society Museum

The state's official historical research organization holds vast collections of photos, books, manuscripts, maps, rare prints, and fine and decorative arts, some dating as far back as the 1600s. ◈ *678 Mission Street • Map P5 • (415) 357-1848 • Open noon–5pm Tue–Sun • Donations*

9 Contemporary Jewish Museum (CJM)

Founded in 1984, this dynamic museum was designed by architect Daniel Libeskind and incorporates the landmark Jesse Street Power Substation. Its exhibitions help to foster relations with the wider community. ◈ *736 Mission St between 3rd and 4th • Map P5 • (415) 655-7800 • Open 1–8pm Thu, 11am–5pm Fri–Tue • Closed Wed, Jewish hols & some public hols • Dis. access • Adm • www.thecjm.org*

10 Metreon

The main attraction at this shopping center is a state-of-the-art cineplex (including IMAX screens), where you can take in the very latest movies' special effects. On the upper deck is a pleasant terrace with superb views of the surrounding cityscape. ◈ *101 4th St • Map Q4*

Top 10 Notable Constructions South of Market

1. AT&T Park
2. SFMOMA
3. Moscone Center
4. Yerba Buena Center
5. Rincon Center
6. Metreon
7. South Park
8. The Galleria
9. Ed Hardy San Francisco
10. The Four Seasons and the Marriott hotels

The Rise of South of Market

Formerly a doggedly industrial area full of warehouses and factories, this flat stretch attracted few residents. For nearly 100 years, it was considered unattractive, if not downright dangerous. All that began to change in the 1970s, when slums were cleared away and the Moscone Center was built. Upscale interior designer showrooms soon followed, ensuing decades brought premier nightclubs, and, the digital boom added more than virtual life to the place. Public structures have sprung up, and the whole district is now seen as a desirable neighborhood – at least for creative types.

Esplanade, South of Market

Mission Dolores

The old Misión San Francisco de Asís acquired its popular name, Mission Dolores, from a small stream that once flowed nearby, Arroyo de Nuestra Señora de los Dolores. It is the oldest building in the city of San Francisco and the oldest intact mission chapel in the chain of 21 (of which it was the sixth) established under the direction of Franciscan friar Father Junipero Serra. The site was founded in 1776, and the chapel was built in 1782–91, with the labor of Ohlone Indians. Its adobe walls are 4 ft (1.2 m) thick and its red-tile roofs are typical of the "Mission Style" which can be seen all over California in both old and new buildings. Reportedly, 36,000 handmade and sun-dried adobe bricks were needed to complete the structure.

Chapel and Basilica façades

🔾 For a fresh, authentic taste of Mexico, head for Pancho Villa Taqueria *(see p113).*

🌀 Check out the old photos in the covered walkway on the right side of the chapel, which depict, among other things, early Indian festivals and the total destruction in 1906 of the church next door, which was replaced by the basilica.

• 3321 16th St at Dolores St
• Map F5
• (415) 621-8203
• www.missiondolores. org • Open 9am–4pm daily • Dis. access
• Suggested donation $5 adult, $3 child

Top 10 Features

1. Cemetery and Serra Statue
2. Chapel
3. Altarpieces
4. Beamed Ceiling Decoration
5. Diorama and Museum
6. Mission Façade
7. Stations of the Cross
8. Choir Windows of St Francis
9. Dolores Street
10. Dolores Park

1 Cemetery and Serra Statue

This historic cemetery *(above)* is the resting place of 5,000 Indians who built the Mission, as well as many of San Francisco's early leaders. Central to the space is a life-size sculpture of Father Junipero Serra.

2 Chapel

The central building *(right)* still retains the original redwood beams, lashed together with rawhide. The amber-colored window glass gives the interior warmth, reflected off gold-leafed fixtures.

3 Altarpieces

The hand-carved, gilded and painted wooden reredos and side altars *(above)* were brought from Mexico in the late 1700s and early 1800s.

For more churches in the city **See pp44–5**

4 Beamed Ceiling Decoration
The imaginative painted ceiling design derives from Ohlone basketry.

5 Diorama and Museum
Just outside the chapel is a diorama showing what life was like at the mission 200 years ago. A museum at the back of the chapel contains artifacts and reproductions of Indian life.

7 Stations of the Cross
These images depicting each of the 14 Stations of the Cross *(above)*, and located throughout the Basilica, were created by the artisan Samuel Berger.

8 Choir Windows of St Francis
At the rear of the basilica, jewel-like stained-glass windows depict scenes from the life of Saint Francis of Assisi, revolutionary patron saint of San Francisco. The lower side windows depict the 21 California Missions.

9 Dolores Street
Undulating like a rollercoaster, this is one of the loveliest streets in San Francisco. Palm trees grace its center all the way along *(above)*.

Plan of Mission Dolores

10 Dolores Park
One of the few large green spaces in the Mission District, this park is situated high on a hill and affords excellent views of the city. It was originally the site of San Francisco's main Jewish cemetery, but was transformed in 1905.

Junipero Serra and California's Missions

In 1769, Gaspar de Portola led an expedition to establish missions in California, with Father Junipero Serra and 60 men. They founded Mission San Diego, and then worked their way up to Monterey. Continuing up the coast, within seven years Father Serra had established a mission in San Francisco, with Father Francisco Palou. In all, Serra founded nine missions in Upper California between 1769 and 1784. His successors founded 12 missions between 1786 and 1823.

6 Mission Façade
The modest white façade of the chapel *(right)* is typical of the Mission Style. Its four columns support niches for three bronze bells, which are inscribed with their names and dates. They were added to the mission in the late 18th century.

⛤10 The Wine Country

The world-famous Wine Country comprises two picturesque valleys, Napa and Sonoma, and the extensive hills and dales surrounding them. Altogether, this bucolic zone boasts over 300 wineries, from which countless award-winning wines have emerged. Napa, the slightly more distant of the two, is more developed for visitors, while Sonoma is more low-key but equally inviting. Both are convenient for a day trip, but it's worth spending a day or two here – not only to sample the fruit of the vine but also to take a dip in one of the rejuvenating hot springs that abound throughout the area (see pp34–5).

Napa Valley sign

🍴 For very special snacks try the Model Bakery at 1357 Main Street in St Helena.

• Napa Valley Wine Train: 1275 McKinstry St, Napa; (707) 253-2111; www.winetrain.com
• Clos Pegase: 1060 Dunaweal Lane; (707) 942-4981; www.clospegase.com • Sterling Vineyard: 1111 Dunaweal Lane; (800) 726-6136; www.sterlingvineyards.com • Opus One: 7900 St Helena Hwy; (707) 944-9442; www.opusonewinery.com
• Domaine Chandon: 1 California Drive, Yountville; (707) 944-2280; www.chandon.com
• Hess Collection: 4411 Redwood Rd, Napa; (707) 255-1144; www.hesscollection.com
• V Sattui: 1111 White Lane, St Helena; (707) 963-7774; www.vsattui.com • Beringer Vineyards: 2000 Main St, St Helena; (707) 963-4812; www.beringer.com • "Old Faithful": 1299 Tubbs Lane, Calistoga; (707) 942-6463; Adm $6–$12; www.oldfaithfulgeyser.com

Top 10 Sights

1. Napa Valley Train
2. Sonoma
3. Clos Pegase
4. Sterling Vineyard
5. Opus One
6. Domaine Chandon
7. Hess Collection
8. V Sattui
9. Beringer Vineyards
10. "Old Faithful" Geyser

Napa Valley Train
Leaving from Napa and arriving in St. Helena, or vice versa, you can avoid the traffic and partake of a gourmet meal complemented by local wines. The trip takes 3 hours in total and the train *(above)* features a 1915 Pullman dining car.

Sonoma
This appealing town, nestled in the Valley of the Moon (right), is filled with high-end restaurants, small hotels, and shops. The town also features a State Historic Park with a mission building and structures from the early to mid-1800s.

Clos Pegase
Housed in an award-winning Postmodern structure, this beguiling winery offers free tours and features an extensive collection of modern art. The wine is memorable, too – specialties include Cabernet, Merlot, and Petite Syrah port.

 The Napa Valley Wine Train offers informative wine tours, all including lunch or dinner; tours range from $99 to $234.

Sterling Vineyard
These whitewashed buildings perched on top of a mountain *(above)* can be seen for miles. The self-guided tour is well marked. Notable wines include Cabernet Sauvignon and Merlot.

Hess Collection
The tours here are a pleasure, including not only wine-making facilities but also the owner's private art gallery of contemporary European and American artists. The Cabernet Sauvignon, Merlot and Chardonnay are especially good.

Map of the Wine Country

"Old Faithful" Geyser
One of only three known geysers in the world that erupt with near-perfect regularity *(below)*. Every 40 minutes, it spews boiling water 60 ft (18 m) into the air.

Opus One
Legendary winemaker Robert Mondavi and Baron Philippe de Roths-child have put their skills together to produce Bordeaux-style reds in their state-of-the-art facilities, modeled on the Château Mouton Roths-child winery in France.

Domaine Chandon
Lovely gardens, a fine restaurant, and sweeping views complement the sparkling, champagne-style wines of this Moët Hennessy showcase. The winery produces 500,000 cases every year.

V Sattui
Extensive gardens *(above)* and a gourmet deli make this the ideal place along the main Napa Valley road to stop for a picnic. Also on offer are wine-tastings of lesser products free of charge – you have to pay for reserve tastings.

Beringer Vineyards
The oldest Napa Valley winery, established in 1876, and the most beau-tiful. Tours include a visit to the 1,000-ft (300-m) wine tunnels, which Chinese laborers carved out of volcanic stone.

California Wine
Since 1857, wine-making has been the mainstay of this area. A phylloxera blight in the early 1900s nearly put an end to it all, but Europe was hit harder, and it was resistant California vines that brought back the wine business to parts of Italy, France, and Spain. In 1976 California wines were put on the international map, when they trounced France in a blind taste-test in Paris. Now, many Euro-pean producers have wineries in the valley.

Left **Massage treatment** Right **Indian Springs**

Wine Country Spas

1 Indian Springs
Indian Springs' tradition of purification and healing began over 8,000 years ago, when Native Americans built sweat lodges here over escaping steam. The ancient tradition continues in the historic 1913 bathhouse, restored to pristine condition. Inside, thermal geysers warm volcanic ash in mud baths, and soothing music is played in the treatment rooms. *1712 Lincoln Ave, Calistoga • (707) 942-4913 • www.indianspringscalistoga.com*

2 Calistoga Spa Hot Springs
The inviting Hot Springs provides a setting in which you can make your visit as restful or as active as you like. Facilities include four outdoor mineral water pools, and exercise and aerobics rooms. *1006 Washington St, Calistoga • (707) 942-6269 • www.calistogaspa.com*

Calistoga Spa Hot Springs

3 Mount View Hotel & Spa
A stay in this historic 1917 resort offers various relaxation and rejuvenation possibilities – mud, milk, or herbal baths, aromatherapy steam showers, body-wraps, massages, or facials – geared to individuals or couples. *1457 Lincoln Ave, Calistoga • (707) 942-5789 • www.mountviewhotel.com*

4 Health Spa Napa Valley
In a serene, open-air setting, guests can yield aches and anxiety to a plethora of pampering and invigorating rituals. For some, that may mean a stimulating fitness workout, or a soothing Herbs of the Valley wrap and massage overlooking the tranquil Spa Garden. *1030 Main St, St Helena • (707) 967-8800 • www.napavalleyspa.com*

5 Dr. Wilkinson's Hot Springs
Over half a century of mud and magic are celebrated here. A mud bath consists of volcanic ash, imported peat, and naturally boiling hot-spring water from the source. Designed for maximum heat penetration and buoyancy, this formula is one of Calistoga's most efficacious. The experience lasts from 10 to 12 minutes and is followed by a warm, mineral water shower. Next comes an aromatic bath, then a steam room. A blanket-wrap follows, then a nap and slow cool down. *1507 Lincoln Ave, Calistoga • (707) 942-4102 • www.drwilkinson.com*

Fairmont Sonoma Mission Inn & Spa

watsu and other massages from certified therapists, attend workshops, and hike throughout the 1,700 acres of land. Or, you can simply lie back and relax. ✆ *18424 Harbin Springs Rd, north of Middletown • (707) 987-2477 • www.harbin.org*

6 Fairmont Sonoma Mission Inn & Spa

This famous inn provides an oasis of ultimate indulgence in luxury and refinement. Blessed by natural mineral hot springs, the legendary spa, with inspired architecture and lovely landscaping, exudes understated opulence and serenity. ✆ *100 Boyes Blvd, Boyes Hot Springs • (707) 938-9000 • www.sonomamissioninn.com*

7 The Kenwood Inn and Spa

Nationally acclaimed as one of the Wine Country's most elegant and intimate country inns, the Kenwood consists of lovely guest suites and a full service spa facility. The inn has the ambiance of an Italian country villa in the heart of the Sonoma Valley, situated on a secluded hillside facing over 1,000 acres of vineyards. The spa offers a variety of massage styles, including aromatherapy and Ayurvedic. ✆ *10400 Sonoma Hwy, Kenwood • (707) 833-1293 • www.kenwoodinn.com*

8 Harbin Hot Springs

Harbin Hot Springs is a non-profit retreat and workshop center located to the north of Calistoga. Its alternative clientele travel from around the world to soak in the natural spring pools, bask on sun decks, receive

9 Boon Hotel & Spa

Located in the beautiful Russian River area, this peaceful setting in the Sonoma County Redwoods offers a reinvigorating retreat from modern life. Body treatments include deep-tissue massages, hot-stone massages, and soothing facials with seaweed anti-wrinkle masks. Included in your stay are use of the pool and Jacuzzi, and evening wine-tastings on selected weekends. The restaurant serves Russian River wines, and sources fresh ingredients from local suppliers or from its own garden. ✆ *14711 Armstrong Woods Rd, Guerneville • (707) 869-2721 • www.boonhotels.com*

10 Sonoma Coast Villa

This family-run, bed and breakfast hotel is nestled in the rolling Californian hills. The Mediterranean-style house is located in 60 acres of beautiful pasturelands near Bodega Bay. Accommodation consists of 18 luxurious rooms with marble bathrooms, fireplaces, and private patios. This secluded retreat offers a variety of spa treatments, including massages, reflexology, and aromatherapy. The hotel can recommend more strenuous activities in the area. ✆ *16702 Coast Hwy 1, Bodega • (707) 876-9818 • www.scvilla.com*

Left **The Gold Rush** Right **Native Americans**

🔟 Moments in History

Native Americans
There were settlements in the Bay as early as the 11th century BC, made up of hunters and gatherers who enjoyed a rich diet of seeds, shellfish, and game. Historians group these peoples into the Coast Miwok, the Wintun, and the Ohlone.

Sir Francis Drake
In 1579, the English privateer landed near Point Reyes and claimed Alta California for Queen Elizabeth I. Along with other early explorers of the area, he failed to notice the marvelous bay just inside the straits. England didn't follow up its claim to Northern California, leaving it to the Spanish to conquer.

Spanish Control
About 200 years after Drake's wanderings, Spain got serious about establishing a presence in Alta California. In

Statue of Father Junipero Serra

1776, an expedition led by Juan Bautista de Anza arrived at San Francisco Bay and established the Presidio (fort). A mission was also founded by Father Junipero Serra (see pp30–31).

American Takeover
Impending war with Mexico in the 1840s inspired US leaders to arouse the interest of Bay Area settlers in joining the Union. In 1846, a party of Yankees in Sonoma declared California's independence from Mexico, christening it the Bear Flag Republic. Shortly after, Commodore John Sloat claimed California as US territory.

Gold Rush Days
In 1848 landowner John Sutter noticed a curious glitter in the sediment of the American River in the Sierra Nevada foothills and realized it was gold. Despite attempts to keep the discovery quiet, word leaked out, and businessman Sam Brannan displayed a bottle of gold dust and nuggets for the whole city to see. The subsequent stampede of '49ers turned the city into a boom town overnight.

Wells Fargo
Stagecoaches of Wells Fargo & Co began carrying freight and passengers in 1852, taking full advantage of the momentum set up by the Gold Rush. It was also instrumental in the development of the Pony Express (see p41).

For historic sites in San Francisco See pp38–9

7 **Panama-Pacific Exposition**
Held in 1915 to celebrate the opening of the Panama Canal, the real *raison d'être* for the festivities was that San Franciscans had resurrected their city after the 1906 disaster *(see p94)*.

8 **Bay and Golden Gate Bridges**
The Bay Bridge's inauguration in 1936 heralded the end of the age of ferryboats by linking the city to the East Bay. The inauguration of the Golden Gate Bridge took place a year later *(see pp8–9)*.

Hippie reveller, Summer of Love

9 **"Summer of Love"**
San Francisco counterculture burst forth in the summer of 1967. Hippies were everywhere, and the poetic music that embodied a new way of thinking filled the air. It was a socio-political shift that affected the whole world.

10 **Politics**
California has always been a few steps ahead of the rest of the US. In 1992 it became the first state to send two female Senators to the US Congress, Dianne Feinstein and Barbara Boxer, while Nancy Pelosi was the first female Speaker of the House from 2007–2011.

Top 10 Scandals and Disasters

1 **Native Americans' Near-Extinction**
In the late 1800s Native Americans were hunted down by settlers, with a bounty paid for each scalp.

2 **Gold Rush Lawlessness**
Gold Rush frontier life was so criminal that vigilante justice was proclaimed in the 1850s, leading to secret trials.

3 **1906**
The earthquake and consequent fire devastated much of the city, and 250,000 people were left homeless.

4 **"Bloody Thursday"**
On July 5, 1934, police fired shots at striking longshoremen, leaving two dead.

5 **Howl**
On October 13, 1955, Allen Ginsberg read his revolutionary poem in San Francisco, which was later banned as obscene.

6 **Freedom & Anti-War**
Pro-Civil Rights and anti-Vietnam War riots occurred from 1964 to 1970.

7 **Rock Icons Die**
Part of hippie legend, Janis Joplin and Jimi Hendrix died in 1970.

8 **White's Revenge**
In 1978 ex-Supervisor Dan White shot dead Mayor George Moscone and gay Supervisor Harvey Milk *(see p39)*.

9 **AIDS**
The AIDS epidemic reached overwhelming proportions in the city in the 1980s.

10 **Loma Prieta Earthquake**
In October 1989, the quake destroyed the Victorian center of Santa Cruz *(see p78)* and part of the Bay Bridge.

Left **Fairmont Hotel, Nob Hill** Center **City Hall** Right **Intersection, Haight-Ashbury**

Historic Sites

1 Mission Dolores
The 18th-century Spanish mission, site of the area's earliest settlement, is worth a visit for its tranquility, as well as for the education it provides about the city's early history *(see pp30–31)*.

2 Jackson Square
The area that witnessed the worst misbehavior of the Barbary Coast days contains some of the city's oldest, loveliest buildings. One of the very few areas that were spared in the 1906 conflagration *(see p84)*.

3 Nob Hill
Erstwhile site of the mansions of Golden Age moguls and potentates, from these lofty heights now rise the city's most lavish hotels and the Gothic spires of one of its best-loved cathedrals *(see p83)*.

Jackson Square

4 Fisherman's Wharf
Remnants of the early fishing industry that contributed to San Francisco's growth are still found here, just layered over with a slick veneer of tourism. Fishing boats still come in and deliver their catch of the day, and nature makes its presence known with a colony of sea lions that lounge on the pier *(see pp12–13)*.

5 War Memorial Opera House
This building was inaugurated in 1932 with a performance of Puccini's *Tosca*, giving the art form a permanent home here. Modeled on its European forbears, with a marble lobby, huge chandelier, balconies, and vaulted ceilings, it is dedicated to the memory of World War I soldiers. In 1945 the Opera House hosted the plenary sessions that preceded the founding of the United Nations and, in 1951, it was the site of the signing of the peace treaty between the US and Japan *(see p56)*.

6 North Beach
The entire area resonates with the history of the early Italian residents, but even more with the iconoclastic legacy of the revolutionary Beats, who brought the neighborhood world-wide fame. Historic churches stand as clear landmarks, while equally historic saloons and cafés take a little snooping around to find *(see p83)*.

For more moments in San Francisco's history **See pp36–7**

Café sign, Haight-Ashbury

Haight-Ashbury

The matrix of yet another Bohemian movement that San Francisco has given birth to, this area nurtured idealistic hippies in the late 1960s. They brought international awareness to alternative ways of life, living in harmony with nature *(see p108)*.

Fillmore Auditorium

One of the legendary homes of psychedelic rock during the 1960s. Along with the Avalon Ballroom and the Winterland (both now gone), this is where the San Francisco Sound found its first audience. ✎ *1805 Geary Blvd • Map E3*

City Hall

On November 28, 1978, ex-Supervisor Dan White went to City Hall and assassinated Mayor George Moscone and gay Supervisor Harvey Milk *(see p37)*. In a botched trial, he was convicted of manslaughter, sparking riots *(see p84)*. ✎ *1 Dr. Carlton B. Goodlett Place • Map R1 • Free tours 10am, noon & 2pm Mon–Fri*

Sutro Baths

Built in 1896 by silver magnate Adolph Sutro, these were at one time the world's largest heated swimming pools, overarched by a stunning glass roof. The complex was destroyed by fire in 1966, but you can access the ruins by steps at the Merrie Way parking lot *(see p116)*.

Top 10 Historic Figures

1 Junipero Serra
This 18th-century Spanish cleric traveled up and down California establishing missions, including Mission Dolores *(see p31)*.

2 John C. Fremont
Instrumental in the US annexation of California in the mid-1800s, it was Fremont who dubbed the Bay straits the "Golden Gate".

3 John Muir
Muir was a keen promoter of the National Parks movement. The Muir Woods are named in his honor *(see p78)*.

4 Leland Stanford
One of the "Big Four" who masterminded the Transcontinental railroad also founded Stanford University *(see p125)*.

5 Mark Hopkins
Another of the "Big Four" who struck it super-rich and lived on Nob Hill.

6 Charles Crocker
Another "Big Four" accomplice. The Crocker Galleria recalls his legacy *(see p50–51)*.

7 A.P. Giannini
Founder in 1904 of the Bank of Italy, later the Bank of America, Giannini financed the Golden Gate Bridge.

8 Harvey Milk
The first openly gay politician to become a member of the Board of Supervisors was assassinated in 1978.

9 Dianne Feinstein
One of the movers and shakers of San Francisco politics in recent decades, she became a US Senator in 1992.

10 Jerry Brown
Buddhist monk and former mayor of Oakland, this learned free spirit ran for president.

Left **de Young** Right **Cable Car Museum**

Museums

1 San Francisco Museum of Modern Art

The city's stylish home for 20th-century European and American art and contemporary multimedia works is a sparkling cultural hub in the South of Market area. Its collections span the whole modern spectrum, from proto-Impressionists to cutting-edge digital installations *(see pp26–9)*.

2 California Academy of Sciences

The environmentally friendly architecture of the Academy building, which emphasizes ecological and sustainable features, blends with the park's natural surroundings. The museum covers virtually every aspect of the natural world *(see p20 and pp22–3)*.

3 Legion of Honor

This museum, located above Land's End, is one of the city's major venues for pre-modern Western art. It is also a beautiful building in a gorgeous natural setting, so well worth the time it takes to get to. It contains mostly European works, including masterpieces by Rubens, Rembrandt, Georges de la Tour, Degas, Rodin, and Monet. ✪ *Lincoln Park, 34th Ave & Clement St • (415) 750-3600 • Map B3 • Open 9:30am–5:15pm Tue–Sun • Dis. access • Adm • www.thinker.org*

The Shades by Auguste Rodin, the Legion of Honor

4 de Young

The old de Young was too damaged in the 1989 earthquake to be saved, but this state-of-the-art facility now houses the museum's extensive collection, which includes 19th-century and contemporary American sculpture and art, and pre-Columbian, African, and Oceanic works. ✪ *50 Hagiwara Tea Garden Drive, Golden Gate Park • Map D4 • (415) 750-3600 • Open 9:30am–5:15pm Tue–Sun, until 8:45pm Fri • Closed major public hols • Dis. access • Adm • www.thinker.org*

Mexican figure, de Young

5 Asian Art Museum

The Asian Art Museum is set in the entirely restructured and seismically retrofitted old Main Library in the Civic Center. The vast and important collection of Chinese, Korean, Japanese, Himalayan, and

Discover more at www.dk.com

Southeast Asian works is displayed by country of origin. But the layout also demonstrates the flow and transformation of Buddhist art from India and outward into the entire Far East. Included is the fabulous Avery Brundage collection of Oriental jade. ◈ 200 Larkin St • Map R2 • (415) 581-3500 • Open 10am–5pm Tue–Sun (10am–9pm Thu) • Adm • www.asianart.org

San Francisco Museum of Craft and Design

This one-of-a-kind museum, celebrates and promotes contemporary craft and design through a variety of innovative exhibitions and educational programs. They organize many lectures, special shows, and programs to engage children, all designed to stimulate creativity. There is also a great museum store with many original, handmade pieces for sale. ◈ 2569 Third St • Map H5 • www.sfmcd.org (check the website for further details)

Cable Car Museum

This brick, warehouse-like structure houses the nuts and bolts machinery that keeps the entire cable car system operating. Don't miss a look downstairs at the giant, spool-like sheaves winding the fat cables round and round (see p11).

Musée Mécanique and Holographic Museum

A quaint, time-warp experience awaits you here. As you approach the lower level, you'll be greeted by the loud guffaws of Laughing Sal, the enormous, buxom figure that is a relic of the old Playland at the Beach. There are also many other often ingenious mechanical devices that once crowded the arcade.

Don't miss the re-creation in miniature of a Chinese opium den. In addition, there is a small collection devoted to the art of holography. ◈ Pier 45, Fisherman's Wharf • Map A3 • Open 10am–7pm Mon–Fri, 10am–8pm Sat–Sun • (415) 346-2000 • Free • www.museemechanique.org

Society of California Pioneers

This museum has fascinating historical exhibits of 19th- and 20th-century California. The upstairs gallery features an annually rotating exhibition of items from their private collection. ◈ 300 4th St • Map R5 • (415) 957-1849 • Open 9am–noon Tue–Fri • Adm • www.californiapioneers.org

Wells Fargo History Museum

The Wells Fargo stagecoaches are the stuff of legends, above all for the tales of their stalwart drivers and the robbers who held them up. Visitors can hear how it must have been to sit on little more than a buckboard for days by listening to the recorded diary of one Francis Brocklehurst. Other exhibits include Pony Express mail, gold nuggets, and photos, and Emperor Norton's currency (see p54). ◈ 420 Montgomery St • Map N5 • Open 9am–5pm Mon–Fri • (415) 396-2619 • Free • www.wells fargohistory.com/museums

Bronze stagecoach (1984), Wells Fargo History Museum

Visit the first museum of gay, lesbian, bisexual, and transgender history (GLBT) in the US. Visit www.glbthistory.org for details

Left **Gallery Wendi Norris** Right **San Francisco Arts Commission Gallery**

🔟 Art Galleries

1 Fraenkel Gallery

One of the gallery's first exhibitions was of NASA's lunar photographs, and this set a tone for what followed. Soon came exhibitions by Eugene Atget, Edward Weston and Diane Arbus, and later, the Bechers, Adam Fuss, and Sol LeWitt. Projects have brought together work across all media, juxtaposing photography with painting, drawing, and sculpture. Other photographers whose work is regularly shown include Richard Avedon and Man Ray. 🔇 *49 Geary St • Map P4 • (415) 981-2661 • Open 10:30am–5:30pm Tue–Fri, 11am–5pm Sat • Free*
• *www.fraenkelgallery.com*

2 City Art Gallery

Owned and operated by the artists themselves, this cooperative gallery prides itself on making artwork accessible and affordable to those interested in collecting art. Showcasing the work of around 200 local artists – some new, some known and established – the gallery exhibits an array of styles and media. Eighty percent of any sale goes directly to the artist. 🔇 *828 Valencia St between 19th & 20th • Map F5 • (415) 970-9900 • Open noon–9pm Wed–Sun • Free*
• *www.cityartgallery.org*

3 Gallery Wendi Norris

This dynamic and extremely stylish contemporary art venue hosts exhibitions of celebrated American and international works, including those by prominent artists from China, Japan, South Korea, and Russia. Some Bay Area artists are also featured in the gallery. The staff provide advice to amateur and serious collectors alike about the contemporary art market. 🔇 *161 Jessie St • Map P3 • (415) 346-7812 • Open 11am–6pm Tue–Sat • Free*
• *www.freynorris.com*

4 Pacific Heritage Museum

Occupying the old San Francisco Mint (1875–7), on top of which the East West Bank has been built. The bank sponsors the museum, which focuses on the art of the Pacific Rim, aiming to bring the work of Asian artists to a wider audience. Exhibitions feature many pieces on loan from private collections. 🔇 *608 Commercial St • Map N5 • (415) 399-1124 • Open 10am–4pm Tue–Sat • Free*

5 Museo ItaloAmericano

A museum, gallery, and community center for San Francisco's Italians. Regular changing temporary exhibitions might focus on the work of either an individual Italian artist, or on aspects of Italian culture. Classes are also offered at the center on Italian art history, culture, architecture, and cookery. 🔇 *Fort Mason Center, Bldg C • Map F1 • (415) 673-2200 • Open noon–4pm daily (Mon by appointment only) • www.museoitaloamericano.org*

Galería de la Raza

Bi-monthly exhibitions of Mexican-American art might include painters, cartoonists, performance artists, muralists, or digital installations. Programs also include films, panel discussions, and performances by stars of the Latino art and music scene. ⊗ 2857 24th St • Map G5 • (415) 826-8009 • Open noon–6pm Tue–Sat • Free • www.galeriadelaraza.org

Intersection for the Arts

Radical and diverse art emerges out of this hotbed of creativity. The alternative multi-genre art installation combines live drama performances, video and film screenings, and panel discussions, which explore the influence of race and relationships on people's work and lives. ⊗ 925 Mission St at 5th St • Map G3 • (415) 626-2787 • Open noon–6pm Tue–Sat • Free • www.theintersection.org

San Francisco Arts Commission Gallery

Opened in 1970 this was one of the first galleries dedicated to showing the work of emerging Bay Area artists. In addition, the Gallery Slide Registry contains images by more than 500 professional artists from across the US. ⊗ 401 Van Ness Ave • Map R1 • (415) 554-6080 • Open noon–5pm Wed–Sat • Free • www.sfartscommission.org/gallery

SoMarts Cultural Center

Group and solo shows, music, and readings all take place here. Founded in 1975, SoMarts is a city-owned cultural center with two exhibition spaces, a 250-seat theater, and printmaking, photography, and design studios. ⊗ 934 Brannan St bet 8th & 9th sts • Map G4 • (415) 863-1414 • Open noon–7pm Tue–Fri, noon–5pm Sat • Free • www.somarts.org

Cartoon Art Museum

Cartoon Art Museum

With an endowment from Peanuts creator, the late Charles M. Schulz, the museum is the only one in the US dedicated to cartoon art in all its forms and has approximately 6,000 pieces. ⊗ 655 Mission St • Map P5 • (415) 227-8666 • Open 11am–5pm Tue–Sun • Adm • www.cartoonart.org

Left **St. John Coltrane's African Orthodox Church** Right **Cathedral of St. Mary of the Assumption**

Churches

1 Grace Cathedral
San Francisco's own Notre Dame combines Italian Renaissance with a lot of American originality *(see pp24–5)*.

2 Mission Dolores
Photos and a diorama offer a stirring impression of what life was like for the Native Americans who built this Spanish mission in the 18th century *(see pp30–31)*.

3 Cathedral of St. Mary of the Assumption
This 1971 building has been compared to a giant washing machine; inside is equally odd, with stained-glass strips and a sculpture of aluminum rods *(see p47)*. ✆ *1111 Gough St • Map F3 • (415) 567-2020 • Services: 6:45am, 8am, 12:10pm Mon–Fri; 6:45am, 8am Sat; 7:30am, 9am, 11am, 1pm (Spanish), 5:30pm Sun • Dis. access • Free*

4 Glide Memorial United Methodist Church
This church has a credo of "the human condition first, not the Bible." Services can draw up to

Grace Cathedral

1,500 celebrants, with a gospel choir. This is also one of the religious institutions where same-sex couples can exchange vows of matrimony. ✆ *330 Ellis St • Map Q3 • (415) 674-6000 • Services: 9am & 11am Sun • Free • www.glide.org*

5 St. John Coltrane's African Orthodox Church
"My music is the spiritual expression of what I am." So said famous jazz musician, St. John Coltrane. Services consist of a performance of Coltrane's "A Love Supreme," by the band Ohnedaruth and the Sisters of Compassion choir. ✆ *St Paul's Lutheran Church, 1286 Fillmore St • Map F3 • (415) 673-7144 • Services: noon Sun • Free • www.coltranechurch.org*

6 First Unitarian Universalist Church
Since 1850, this church has been a progressive voice in the city. Welcoming all faiths and creeds, this congregation is not bound by dogma, but by shared values. ✆ *1187 Franklin St • Map P1 • (415) 776-4580 • Services: 11am Sun • Free • www.uusf.org*

7 St. Mark's Lutheran Church
This 1894 pink-brick church is a mix of Gothic and Romanesque styles. After the 1906 earthquake *(see p37)*, it served as a first-aid station and shelter. ✆ *1111 O'Farrell St • Map P1 • (415) 928-7770 • Services: 6:45pm Wed; 9am & 11am Sun • Free • www.sfmarks-sf.org*

Outside of service times, most churches are open to the public free of charge to look around the buildings.

St. Patrick's Cathedral

Constructed in 1872, this Gothic Revival cathedral has an impressive marble and stained-glass interior. ◉ *756 Mission St • Map Q4 • (415) 421-3730 • Services: 7:30am, 12:10pm, 5:15pm Mon–Sat; 7:30am, 9am, 10:30am, 12:15pm, 5:15pm Sun • Free • www.stpatricksf.org*

Shrine of St. Francis of Assisi

Declared a National Historic Landmark, the Gothic Revival St. Francis of Assisi Church was established on June 17, 1849, as the first parish church in California. The interior is adorned with 11 larger-than-life murals, depicting the works of San Francisco's patron saint. ◉ *610 Vallejo St at Columbus • Map M4 • (415) 986-4557 • Services: 12:15pm Mon–Sat, 10am Sun • Free • www.shrinesf.org*

Sts. Peter & Paul Church

North Beach's landmark "Italian Church" was once dubbed the "Marzipan Church" for the frothy stucco decoration on its soaring pinnacles. Inside, there is a sculpted reproduction of Leonardo da Vinci's *Last Supper (see p88)*.

Sts. Peter & Paul Church

Top 10 Other Places of Worship

1 Kong Chow Temple
The oldest of Chinatown's temples is dedicated to Kuan Di, a male deity *(see pp18–19)*.

2 Tin How Temple
The Queen of Heaven rules this sanctuary and makes sure devotees travel safely by water, among other things *(see pp18–19)*.

3 Temple Sherith Israel
Founded in 1849 by Jewish pioneers, the present domed synagogue dates from 1904. ◉ *2266 California St • Map F3 • Services: 6pm Fri, 10:30am Sat • Free*

4 Vedanta Temple
This was the first Hindu Temple (1905) in the western US. ◉ *2323 Vallejo St • Map M5 • Free*

5 Zen Center
Home to the city's Zen practitioners. ◉ *300 Page St • Map F4*

6 Crystal Way
Healing through crystals, light, sound, and positive thinking are explored here. ◉ *2335 Market St • Map F5*

7 Botanica Yoruba
All the Santeria paraphernalia you'll need *(see p110)*.

8 Spirit Rock Meditation Center
Helps people find peace through meditation. ◉ *5000 Sir Francis Drake Blvd, Woodacre, Marin*

9 The Love of Ganesha
Hindu clothing, arts, and crafts. ◉ *1310 Haight St • Map E4*

10 Open Secret
The backroom of this New Age venue is like a temple to all the world's deities. ◉ *923 C St, San Rafael • Hwy 1*

Left **San Francisco Museum of Modern Art** Right **Palace of Fine Arts**

🔟 Architectural Highlights

1 Transamerica Pyramid
Hated by many at first, the Pyramid is now loved as an icon of the city. Recalling pyramids of ancient cultures, to some it is a symbol of the mysticism that has always played a part in the San Francisco mentality. At 853 ft (260 m), it is the tallest building in the city, but its shape keeps it from casting a shadow on the neighborhood. ⬡ *600 Montgomery St • Map N5*

2 Bank of America
This 52-story structure was the first skyscraper to be erected in the city, in 1972. The color was a mistake – the granite that faces it was supposed to be pink, not brown, but by the time delivery was made, it was too late. ⬡ *555 California St • Map N5*

3 San Francisco Museum of Modern Art
Quoting Renaissance architecture in thoroughly modern ways, SFMOMA has established itself as the city's premier Post-Modern effort. The interior has a flexibility and functionality that works perfectly with the collections displayed *(see pp26–9)*.

4 Coit Tower
Perched on Telegraph Hill, this Art Deco sentinel takes the form of a giant fluted column. Reminiscent of Renaissance towers, the column is 210-ft (64-m) tall and is perforated around the top with arched openings and

windows, which visitors can reach by elevator for stunning views of the city *(see p88)*.

5 Palace of Fine Arts
This bit of Neo-Classical fluff was designed by Bernard Maybeck for the Pan-Pacific Exposition of 1915. It is patterned on an 18th-century engraving by Giovanni Piranesi entitled *The Isle of the Dead (see p94)*.

6 Civic Center
Centered on the City Hall that would do any state proud, the core buildings are in a grand Beaux-Arts style; and befitting the city that started the Gold Rush, gilt is everywhere *(see p84)*.

7 Haas-Lilienthal House
This Queen Anne-style mansion, built in 1886, is one of the few Victorian beauties in the city that accepts callers. It's a wonderful glimpse into the way of life among San Francisco's upper-middle classes from about 1890 to 1920. Outside, it features

Haas-Lilienthal House

For a walking tour of the city's famous Victorian houses, contact (415) 252-9485 or visit www.victorianwalk.com

Transamerica Pyramid

gables, a turret, and patterned embellishments; inside, you can see parlors, a dining room, bedrooms, and a ballroom.
⊗ *2007 Franklin St • Map M1 • (415) 441-3011 • Open noon–3pm Sat & Wed, 11am–4pm Sun • Adm*

Grace Cathedral
Executed in the medieval French Gothic style, echoing in particular Notre Dame in Paris, yet accomplished using steel-reinforced concrete. It is the third largest Episcopal church in the US *(see pp24–5)*.

Xanadu Gallery
Dating from 1948, this is the city's only building by Frank Lloyd Wright. The sweeping spiral ramp predates that at Wright's Guggenheim Museum in New York. ⊗ *140 Maiden Lane • Map P4 • (415) 392-9999 • Open 10am–6pm Tue–Sat • Free • www.folkartintl.com*

St. Mary's Cathedral
Critics abound who are ready to dismiss this parabolic form, but the soaring curves take the attention upward, in much the same fashion that tracery and peaked vaulting do in Gothic cathedrals *(see p44)*.

Top 10 Public Art Sites

1 Balmy Alley
The most famous set of murals in town, by local Latino artists. ⊗ *24th & 25th sts between Harrison and Treat • Map G6*

2 San Francisco Art Institute
Diego Rivera, the Mexican muralist, painted *The Making of a Fresco* here. ⊗ *800 Chestnut St • Map K3*

3 Coit Tower
Depression-era murals decorate the lobby *(see p88)*.

4 Fort Mason
Oliver DiCicco's *Bow Seat* is a homage to all small boats that have worked the Bay. ⊗ *Franklin St • Map J1*

5 Women's Building
The work of seven women painters graces the façade. ⊗ *18th St between Valencia & Guerrero • Map F5*

6 Bikeway
This 340-ft (104-m) mural chronicles a bike-ride from Downtown to Ocean Beach. ⊗ *Duboce St between Church & Market • Map F4*

7 Beach Chalet
Depression-era murals depict famous citizens. ⊗ *1000 Great Hwy • Map A4*

8 Rincon Center
These 1948 murals by Russian artist Anton Refregier trace Californian history. ⊗ *Mission, Howard, Steuart & Spear sts • Map H2*

9 Financial District
The black-stone *Transcendence* is in front of the Bank of America.

10 Golden Gate Park
The Music Concourse has bronzes, including *Apple Cider Press (see pp20–21)*.

➜ There are walking and biking tours showcasing murals in the Mission District. Contact (415) 285-2287 for details.

47

Left **Embarcadero Park** Right **Buena Vista Park**

🔟 Parks and Gardens

Golden Gate Park
One of the largest city parks in the US is also one of the most diverse, and all of it brought forth from what was once scrub and dunes. The park also features first-rate cultural attractions such as the de Young Museum (see pp20-21).

Buena Vista Park
This steep and densely wooded hill offers terrific panoramas from its Haight Street location, as well as some fairly challenging trails for those who like to hike and bike. ✎ Map E4

Fort Mason
The rolling lawn above Fort Mason Center (see p94), known as the Great Meadow, is a relatively little-used park, but it's great for taking a siesta, tossing a frisbee, or just strolling through to take in the spectacular views from the cliffs. ✎ Map F1

Shakespeare Garden, Golden Gate Park

The Presidio
This vast swathe of greenery only entered the city's repertoire of parklands in 1994. It is a beautiful public space and many tourists and city inhabitants come to enjoy the wooded areas, walking trails, and wonderful views over the Bay. It is also home to chic restaurants and museums. Filmmaker George Lucas has created a $350 million headquarters here for his production company LucasFilm and up to 1,500 employees.

Alta Plaza
Pacific Heights's double block of verdant hill is a popular place to take the sun when it ventures to break through the fog. Basketball and tennis courts and a children's playground are in the center, while to the south there are terraced lawns, onto which some of Pacific Heights' oldest homes face. ✎ Map E2

Alamo Square
Postcard central, thanks to its row of perfect Victorians backed by the knock-out Downtown view. The park itself is a sloping patch of green, while the surrounding streets are lined with so many grand old houses that it has been declared a historic site. Two of them have been turned into hotels, although the areas immediately outside the square are not the most salubrious at night. ✎ Map E4

Note: San Francisco's parks should generally be avoided at night.

Embarcadero Park

The last few years have witnessed a welcome transformation along the entire stretch of the Embarcadero. The 1989 earthquake put an end to the idea of running a freeway into the city center, so the old shipping piers are now set off by greenery and sidewalks, and the area is being promoted as a breezy park. In-line skaters and cyclists disport themselves where concrete embankments once held sway (see p93).

Yerba Buena Gardens

A small but very welcome patch of green in an otherwise paved-over area. When the weather is fine, the lawn is populated by sunbathers, while other parts of the gardens feature beautiful memorial fountains and sculptures (see p28).

Lafayette Park

This is another of Pacific Heights's double-blocked hilltop gardens – a leafy green haven of pine and eucalyptus. Steep stairways lead to the summit, with its delightful views. The city did not manage to set aside

Lafayette Park

these oases without a fight. Squatters' buildings occupied some of the land in the center of this park until as late as 1936, when they were finally pulled down, liberating the lush gardens for all to enjoy. ◈ Map F2

Walton Park

This tiny park is a much needed break from concrete and asphalt for Downtown workers, whom you will see picnicking here at weekday lunchtimes. The park evokes a peaceful mountain meadow. A wonderful sculpture by Georgia O'Keeffe adds contrast, while a central fountain sends droplets of water falling across cement blocks below. ◈ Map M6

Left **Gump's** Right **Embarcadero Center**

Stores and Shopping Centers

1 Gump's
Founded in 1861 by German immigrants, this homegrown department store has one of the largest collections in the US of fine china and crystal, selling famous names such as Baccarat, Lalique, and Georg Jensen silver. For more designer options continue down Post Street to Crocker Galleria ⊗ *135 Post St • Map P4*

2 Nordstrom
Located on the top five floors of the Westfield Center, the fashion emporium is known as the "store in the sky." Impeccable service, a vast selection, and a refined atmosphere featuring live piano music make this a very upscale shopping experience. ⊗ *San Francisco Shopping Center, 865 Market St • Map Q4*

3 Neiman Marcus
This high-end store overlooks Union Square from a plum spot once occupied by the City of Paris building, constructed in

Nordstrom

the 1890s but torn down to build this modern structure. Part of the original remains, however, by way of the huge stained-glass dome. Neiman's boast is that it can get anything you might want. Lunch in the rotunda is the least expensive way to experience the store. ⊗ *150 Stockton St • Map P4*

4 Saks Fifth Avenue
For decades, the name has been synonymous with high style and this branch of the New York mainstay is one of the best embodiments of the store's mythic elan. You'll find just about every international designer of note here. ⊗ *384 Post St • Map P4*

5 Macy's
This old-guard department store has become an all-purpose emporium carrying merchandise in all price ranges. During the Christmas holidays, the window displays are well worth a visit. ⊗ *170 O'Farrell St • Map P4*

6 Barney's New York
This store comprises four full stories of style in Union Square. It's the place to go for both men and women to find those must-have designer clothes, shoes, and accessories from the likes of Marc Jacobs and Comme des Garcons. It also boasts the best fragrance department in the city. Just be prepared to pay handsomely for all those clothes. ⊗ *77 O'Farrell St • Map G3*

 For tips on shopping in San Francisco **See p140**

Crocker Galleria

Embarcadero Center

Four low-rise blocks connect to form this sprawling, outdoor shopping center. Dominated by chain stores like Gap, it's probably not the place to find a unique souvenir. The upper floors host restaurants and a movie theater. ◎ *Embarcadero & Battery, Sacramento & Clay sts • Map N6*

Ghirardelli Square

Housing over 20 restaurants and shops, this former chocolate factory has become one of the most frequented destinations in Fisherman's Wharf. The stores range from tourist T-shirt shops to fine jewelry boutiques *(see p13)*. ◎ *900 North Point St • Map K1*

Ferry Building Marketplace

Feast on specialties from around the Bay and take home regional chocolates and olive oil. ◎ *Embarcadero at Market • Map H2*

Westfield Shopping Center

This center has ten levels and nearly 400 stores, including Bloomingdale's, a movie theater and gourmet food area. ◎ *865 Market St • Map Q4*

Top 10 Shopping Areas

1 Union Square
Traditionally the focal point of all the best stores, including Tiffany & Co, Armani, Prada, Cartier, Yves St Laurent, Chanel, and more *(see p84)*.

2 Union Street
Converted Victorian homes house a charming assortment of boutiques, bookstores, antiques shops, restaurants, and a cinema *(see p99)*.

3 Grant Avenue
The southernmost four blocks are chic shopping off Union Square; then you enter eight blocks of exotic Chinatown emporiums; finally, Upper Grant is all about North Beach hangouts. ◎ *Map N4*

4 Upper Fillmore Street
A colorful choice of cafés, restaurants, and boutiques, all geared to a high-end Pacific Heights clientele. ◎ *Map E2*

5 Market Street
A good place to find cut-rate electronics shops, outlet shops, and the Westfield Mall. ◎ *Map Q3*

6 Hayes Valley
These blocks offer galleries and stores with an avant-garde feel *(see p100)*.

7 Chestnut Street
Clothing boutiques, health-food shops, and an old-fashioned cinema. ◎ *Map K1*

8 The Mission
Plenty of super-discount stores and funky home furnishing shops *(see p108)*.

9 Castro Street
Fine shops, gay bookstores and erotic boutiques *(see p107)*.

10 Haight Street
The place for secondhand clothing, emporiums, and the best shoe stores *(see p99)*.

Left **Jack London** Right **Dashiell Hammett**

Top 10 Writers

1 Jack London
Adventurer and author of frontier tales such as *White Fang*, *The Sea Wolf*, and *The Call of the Wild*, Jack London (1876–1916) grew up in Oakland. There a museum of his memorabilia is housed in a reconstruction of the log cabin he lived in while prospecting for gold in the Yukon Territory. His fiction is based on his experiences in the untamed West and the social inequality he saw in boom town San Francisco.

2 Dashiell Hammett
The author of *The Maltese Falcon* and creator of the classic hard-boiled detective Sam Spade made San Francisco his home from 1921 to 1929. He used the fog-swirled slopes of the city's hills as the perfect backdrop for his stylish crime stories. Hammett (1894–1961) was himself employed briefly at the famous Pinkerton Detective Agency.

3 Gertrude Stein & Alice B. Toklas
Stein (1874–1946) was raised in Oakland, Toklas (1877–1967) in San Francisco, and both were members of the wealthy Jewish bourgeoisie that has played such an important part in the city's cultural life. But these two larger-than-life women soon deserted the Bay Area for Paris, where they became Queen Bees of a circle of brilliant international artists and writers, including Pablo Picasso and Ernest Hemingway.

4 Jack Kerouac
Arriving from New York in 1947, it was Kerouac (1922–69) who coined the term "Beat." He and his companions – Neal Cassady, Allen Ginsberg, Lawrence Ferlinghetti, and others – initiated the new politics of dissent and free love, all of which led, within a decade, to the Hippie Movement *(see p37)*. His classic novel *On the Road* (1957) galvanized a generation.

5 Allen Ginsberg
Ginsberg (1926–97) cleared the way for the eventual Gay Liberation Movement by openly declaring his homosexuality in his literary milestone *Howl*, first unveiled to the public in 1955 *(see p37)*. His epic poem soon attracted charges of obscenity in the buttoned-down, witch-hunting 1950s. Ginsberg's spiritual mysticism also set the tone for the Hippie Movement.

Jack Kerouac

Armistead Maupin

Top 10 Movies Set in San Francisco

1 San Francisco
Clark Gable and Jeannette Macdonald star in this 1936 film set amid the rubble of the 1906 earthquake.

2 The Maltese Falcon
Classic Bogart (1941), in which he embodies detective Sam Spade. The four-year-old Bay Bridge is in evidence.

3 Dark Passage
This Humphrey Bogart and Lauren Bacall vehicle (1947) makes use of San Francisco's moody climate.

4 Vertigo
A classic Alfred Hitchcock thriller (1958) memorably shows the crashing waves under Golden Gate Bridge.

5 Bullitt
Probably the most famous car-chase ever filmed, due to the city's infamous hills (1968).

6 Armistead Maupin
Maupin's *Tales of the City* were serialized in the *San Francisco Chronicle* before being published in book form. They are lighthearted paeans to the idiosyncrasies of gay San Francisco in the 1970s, before the specter of AIDS changed everything.

6 Dirty Harry
Yet another detective story (1971) set in the city that invites such mysteries, perhaps due to its fog.

7 Alice Walker
African-American feminist and dedicated San Franciscan, Walker's novel *The Color Purple* (1982) set the tone for a new vision of black heritage, as seen from the woman's point of view.

7 Invasion of the Body Snatchers
This 1978 remake of the 1950s classic stars Donald Sutherland as the last survivor of a chilling alien takeover.

8 Wallace Stegner
A Stanford professor of creative writing, Stegner's novel *Angle of Repose* won the Pulitzer Prize in 1972.

8 Basic Instinct
This 1992 thriller sees Sharon Stone and Michael Douglas cross Golden Gate Bridge to a love-pad at Seadrift.

9 Amy Tan
When Tan's *The Joy Luck Club* (1989) hit the scene, San Francisco's Chinese community at last found its voice. It illustrated Chinese culture and its clash with uprooted Americana.

9 Mrs Doubtfire
Native San Franciscan Robin Williams is in drag in this 1993 spoof. Golden Gate Park is shown to full effect.

10 Danielle Steele
Steele's "bodice-rippers" have had such success that she can now afford to be mistress of the very finest Pacific Heights mansion *(see p99)*.

10 The Pursuit of Happyness
A 2006 Will Smith drama set in the gritty Tenderloin district.

One of Wallace Stegner's most famous students was Ken Kesey, author of the bestseller One Flew Over the Cuckoo's Nest.

Left **Joshua Abraham Norton** Center **Joan Baez** Right **Willie Brown**

🔟 Eccentric & Noteworthy Characters

1 Sally Sanford

The Sausalito Chart House Restaurant is the former purview of Sally Sanford (1903–82), the one-time bawdy house doyenne, and then Honorary Mayor of Sausalito. Since Gold Rush days, San Francisco has loved and even honored those who stand for the city's sexual liberality.

2 Joshua Abraham Norton

Born in 1819, Norton made his fortune in San Francisco but lost it all in 1852. The event left him unhinged but harmless, and he declared himself "Emperor of the United States and Protector of Mexico." He issued his own money, and was lovingly indulged by the city's populace until his death in 1880.

3 Jello Biafra

Punk rock lead vocalist for The Dead Kennedys, Biafra ran for mayor of San Francisco in 1979. His basic belief was that corrupt governments and corporations should be fought, not trusted. He chose the name Jello Biafra because of "the way the two images collide in people's minds," with "Jello" as the embodiment of American blandness and "Biafra" as the universal symbol of starvation. His platform included having businessmen wear clown suits to the office. He finished fourth out of a field of ten, with 3.5 per cent of the total votes.

Jello Biafra and The Dead Kennedys

4 Sister Boom-Boom

One of the original Sisters of Perpetual Indulgence, a self-described order of gay male nuns, Sister Boom-Boom took part in street theater with them in the late 1970s and early 1980s. In 1982 he ran for a seat on the Board of Supervisors of San Francisco, winning 23,125 votes. He is also a recognized astrologer and uses New Age science to interpret gay issues for the community.

5 Melvin Belli

Known as the "King of Torts", the flamboyant Belli was a pivotal figure in fostering today's litigious society as an innovator in the area of personal injury law. He took on big corporations and controversial clients, including Errol Flynn, Jim and Tammy Faye Bakker, Lana Turner, Mae West, Muhammad Ali, and Jack Ruby. Belli died in 1996 at the age of 88, just a few months after filing for bankruptcy.

6 Joan Baez

Known in her youth as "The Voice," girlfriend of Bob Dylan, and peacenik, the Palo Alto native later came out as a lesbian, continuing to work for peace and social justice. In 2001, Baez created a cabaret character, the Contessa ZinZanni, in a show that has enjoyed good reviews in San Francisco.

7 Mrs. Madrigal

Olympia Dukakis brought this wonderful *Tales of the City* character to vibrant life in the mini-series based on Armistead Maupin's books *(see p53)*. Anna Madrigal is a transsexual land-lady who rents out apartments to young singles, both gay and straight, and tends to her mari-juana plants and her charges with equal wisdom and spirituality.

8 Francis Ford Coppola

The director of *The Godfather* makes San Francisco the home of his Zoetrope productions, and has also branched out into other enterprises. His Niebaum-Coppola winery in the Napa Valley is one of the best.

9 Herb Caen

For nearly six decades Caen's newspaper column was required reading. To his many devoted fans he was, and remains "Mr. San Francisco." He coined the term "Beatnik" in his April 2, 1958, column.

10 Willie Brown

San Francisco's first African-American mayor was famous for his *bon vivant* ways. His high-living, fast-shuffling style did not detract from his popularity, however, and the city seemed to prosper under his tutelage.

Top 10 Sixties Figures

1 Janis Joplin

This troubled singer from Texas became the queen of the San Francisco sound, until her death by heroin overdose.

2 Ken Kesey

A powerful, revolutionary writer, his Magic Bus and Trips Festival set the tone for the entire Hippie Movement.

3 Jerry Garcia

Patriarch of the San Francisco sound, his Grateful Dead band continued to tour until his death in 1995.

4 Mario Savio

The UC Berkeley student launched the Free Speech Movement on the campus in the late 1960s.

5 Owsley Stanley

The most famous source of pure LSD in the 1960s.

6 Grace Slick

The other queen of San Francisco's influential bands, in this case Jefferson Airplane.

7 Huey Newton

Oakland's founder of the Black Panthers, a group committed to violent change if necessary.

8 Patty Hearst

The newspaper heiress, kidnapped by the Symbionese Liberation Army in 1974, apparently converted and took part in an armed robbery.

9 Jim Jones

The leader of a Fillmore District religious group who moved en masse to South America ended his days and those of some 900 followers in 1978, in a mass suicide by cyanide-laced Kool-Aid.

10 Charles Manson

This commune leader and his followers murdered actress Sharon Tate in 1969.

Left **Louise M. Davies Symphony Hall** Right **War Memorial Opera House**

Performing Arts Venues

War Memorial Opera House and San Francisco Ballet

The San Francisco Opera Company is the second largest in the country and performs from June to January. The excellent San Francisco Ballet, one of the nation's oldest, mostly performs at the Opera House, too *(see p84)*. ✪ *301 Van Ness Ave • Map R1 • (415) 864-3330*

Louise M. Davies Symphony Hall

With performances from September to May, under the directorship of Michael Tilson Thomas, the San Francisco Symphony Orchestra performs in this modern structure with carefully modulated acoustics. Built in 1980, this curving, glass-fronted concert hall is loved and loathed in equal measure by San Franciscans. Its corner placement is set off by a Henry Moore bronze, which also has its share of detractors. ✪ *201 Van Ness Ave • Map R1 • (415) 864-6000*

Masonic Auditorium

Originally a Masonic Temple, built in 1957, this attractive structure, with its 3,000-seat auditorium, is used as a venue for jazz performances, lectures, and readings, as well as conventions and seminars. Mosaics inside and out depict some of the tenets of Freemasonry. ✪ *1111 California St • Map N3 • (415) 776-7457*

Curran Theater

Built in 1922, this is one of the grandest theaters in the city and a Registered National Historic Landmark. The interior is a fantasy of gold and carved wood, complemented by a vast chandelier and murals. Shows tend toward long-running Broadway hits. ✪ *445 Geary St • Map P3 • (415) 551-2000 • www.shnsf.com*

Golden Gate Theater

This former movie house, designed with Moorish influences in the 1920s, is one of the city's larger mainstream theaters. Its usual offerings are traveling Broadway blockbusters, such as *Wicked*, *West Side Story*, and Monty Python's *Spamalot*. ✪ *1 Taylor St • Map Q3 • (415) 551-2000 • www.shnsf.com*

SFJAZZ Center

With specially designed acoustics and an intimate concert hall, the luminous building that houses the SFJAZZ Center is the first in the US to be specifically built for jazz

San Francisco Symphony Orchestra

 If you want to see some of the most popular shows in San Francisco, it is always wise to book well in advance.

Orpheum

performances. The Center aims to educate and inspire audiences with an eclectic program of events from world-class musicians. ⊗ *205 Franklin St at Fell St • Map R1 • (866) 920-5299*

Orpheum
Originally a vaudeville house and then a movie theater, this is the historic spot where *Hair* was given its first West Coast performance some three decades ago – known locally as "the New York version of what happened here in San Francisco." The theater, decorated in 1920s Moorish taste, now mostly stages Broadway shows. ⊗ *1192 Market St • Map R2 • (415) 551-2000 • www.shnsf.com*

American Conservatory Theater (ACT)
Founded in the 1960s, San Francisco's most important theater company is internationally respected and has produced premieres of a number of major plays. At the heart of ACT is one of the most acclaimed actor-training institutions in the nation – former students include Denzel Washington, Annette Bening, and Winona Ryder. ⊗ *Geary Theater, 415 Geary St • Map P3 • (415) 749-2228 • www.act-sf.org*

Magic Theatre
In the 1970s, none other than Sam Shepard was the resident playwright of the Magic, and its stage has seen performances by the likes of Sean Penn and Nick Nolte. It specializes in bringing new plays to light, usually by up-and-coming Americans. It also offers "raw play" readings of as yet unstaged works. ⊗ *Fort Mason Center, Bldg D • Map F1 • (415) 441-8822 • www.magictheatre.org*

Beach Blanket Babylon
High camp and high head-dresses, along with jolly good singing by the veteran ensemble cast make this one of the joys of the city. It's been zinging the heartstrings of lovers of San Francisco for more than a quarter of a century and shows no signs of flagging. The excuse for all this frivolity is the sending up of various notables, most of whom well deserve the good-natured ribbing. ⊗ *Club Fugazi, 678 Green St • Map L4 • (415) 421-4222*

Left **Golden Gate Park playground** Right **Exploratorium**

🔟 Children's Attractions

Exploratorium

Kids can experience one of the finest, uniquely San Francisco interactive days at this superb science museum at Pier 15. They'll learn all about their senses and how they work, as well as delve into all the laws of physics through first-hand experiments. The top draw, however, is the Tactile Dome, a totally dark sphere in which you feel your way along, touching a range of sensorially stimulating objects and textures *(see p85)*.

Crazy Castle, San Francisco Zoo

San Francisco Zoo

Direct encounters with farm animals and visits with zoo babies, which may include gorillas, snow leopards, rhinos, or alpacas, make this a must-do for the youngsters. Although perhaps not the biggest or best zoo in the world, its attention to top-quality children's programs,

such as the many feeding times and the creepy-crawly insect denizens, make it one of the best for budding zoologists. The landscaping of whole the place, from the Carousel to the natural habitats, is also designed for maximum fun *(see p116)*.

Aquariums

Part of Golden Gate Park's California Academy of Sciences *(see pp22–3)*, the Steinhart Aquarium is a big hit with kids. The darkened corridors are filled with softly glowing tanks in which some of the weirdest creatures on the planet disport themselves. Then there's the Touching Tidal Pool if kids want to get up close and personal with their finny friends. At Fisherman's Wharf, UnderWater World gives an even greater undersea experience, with walk-through transparent tunnels surrounded by sea life *(see p13)*.

Children's Creativity Museum

This elaborate complex, aimed both at entertaining kids and spurring their creativity to the max, is part of the greater Yerba Buena Center. There's an old-fashioned carousel; a labyrinth; a studio where they can script, produce, and star in their own videos; art studios; and a digital workshop, plus lots more to keep them busy all day long. Ages 5 to 18 *(see p28)*.

Alcatraz

Randall Museum

Perched above the city, in Corona Heights Park, this small, welcoming complex is primarily a petting zoo, with farm animals, raccoons, reptiles, and birds. But it also offers hands-on experience with woodworking, pottery, painting, theater, photography, model railroads, storytelling, gardening, and more. The aim is to teach children respect for nature and the environment.
Ⓢ *199 Museum Way, off Roosevelt Way, Buena Vista • Map E4 • (415) 554-9600 • Open 10am–5pm Tue–Sat • Free • www.randallmuseum.org*

Alcatraz

"The Rock" is always a hit with older children, particularly boys, who relate to the grim, quasi-military aspects of the place. The wildness of the island's natural beauty, as well as the ferry ride out and back, will also delight. Smaller kids might find it a bit frightening *(see pp14–17)*.

Bay Area Discovery Museum

This hands-on museum is aimed directly at children. Kids will be able to enjoy an art studio, a science lab, a wave workshop where they learn about sea and plant life, and a media center.
Ⓢ *557 McReynolds Rd, Sausalito • (415) 339-3900 • Open 9am–4pm Tue–Fri, 10am–5pm Sat–Sun • Closed public hols & last two weeks in Sep • Dis. access • Adm • www.baykidsmuseum.org*

Golden Gate Park Playground

At the southeastern corner of the park, kids will love the old carousel, a treehouse, and some great swings, slides, and other kid-driven rides. In the summer, there are often Punch and Judy shows to tickle and delight children of all ages *(see pp20–23)*.

Angel Island State Park

An ideal place for a full-day family outing. You can picnic, swim, hike, kayak, camp, or take the tram tour that goes all around the island, with a guide who points out sites of historic interest – dating from the days when the place was a rather forbidding immigrant clearing station *(see p93)*.

Metreon

Intended as a bustling, high-tech, multilevel amusement arcade for adolescents, so far the only thing that seems to have clicked is the superb multiscreen cinema complex. Here you can watch the latest Hollywood blockbusters with full digital sound effects amped up to the highest possible level. Otherwise, the Metreon offers several different restaurant choices and great views of the city from the fourth floor deck space *(see p29)*.

Angel Island State Park

Left **Divisadero** Right **Twin Peaks**

Scenic Drives

1 49-Mile Drive
This all-in-one driving tour is marked with blue-and-white seagull markers, and winds its way through the most picturesque parts of the city. It can be challenging to follow, keeping an eye out for the markers and the traffic at the same time, but you can get a map of the route from the Visitor Information Center *(see p132)*.

49-Mile Drive marker

2 Mount Tamalpais
The road that leads up to the top of "Mount Tam" is appropriately called Panoramic Highway. All the way along, it provides you with dramatic views of the Marin Headlands, both on the Bay and ocean sides, and as you approach the summit, far-reaching views of the Bay Area *(see p124)*.

3 Conzelman Road
This road hugs the bluffs, high above the waves, on the southern edge of the Marin Headlands. It affords some of the most famously beautiful views of the north tower of Golden Gate Bridge, looking back at the city in the distance. The way is punctuated with old military bunkers, since this entire area was once given over to the army to guard the western shores. ◈ *Marin County*

4 Twin Peaks
More famous panoramas await you here, as you wind your way up the two mountains. You can get 360-degree views of the city to the east, the ocean to the west, the Bay to the north, and the valleys to the south *(see p107)*.

5 The Great Highway
Broad and straight, this coast highway begins at Cliff House at the northern end and eventually meets the famous Highway 1, which takes you, via dramatic cliffs, down to Half Moon Bay, Santa Cruz, Monterey, Carmel, Big Sur – and eventually, to Mexico. ◈ *Map A4*

6 Divisadero
This street cuts a great swathe through the city centre. It starts in the south at Duboce Street, then rises to glorious mansions and Bay vistas after Geary Expressway. ◈ *Map E4*

7 Berkeley & Oakland Hills
Blending gently with the Berkeley Hills, the Oakland Hills offer some beautiful parks, such as Redwood Regional Park. Skyline Boulevard provides access to most of this ridge area, with many picnic groves and hiking options along the winding way. ◈ *Hwy 24*

Skyline Drive

Pick up this bucolic road (Highway 35) at Lake Merced *(see p117)*, and it will take you all the way down the woody spine of the Peninsula to Santa Cruz. It's a total immersion in nature, just minutes from the populated areas around the Bay.

La Honda & Old La Honda Roads

Behind Stanford University *(see p125)* is the quiet town of Portola Valley. From here, these picturesque switchback roads ascend to meet Skyline Drive. They are very narrow in places, and you can't go more than 10 mph (16 kmph), but the timeless beauty of the Bay Area forests makes it worthwhile.

Highway 9 and Big Basin State Park

This gently mountainous region is almost entirely undeveloped. The main town, Boulder Creek, is like a small frontier settlement, where craftspeople sell their wares, and country stores cater mostly to locals. This is an area that time happily forgot.

Highway 1, from The Great Highway

Top 10 Hair-Raising Hills

1 Lombard Street
Called "The Crookedest Street in the World," it isn't too hair-raising, but the views of North Beach as you descend are charming. ⬡ *Map L1*

2 Top of Divisadero
The most dramatic section of Divisadero is the highest point in Pacific Heights. ⬡ *Map E2*

3 Twin Peaks
The view from these peaks seems like one from a helicopter, hovering over the city. ⬡ *Map E6*

4 Gough between Jackson and Washington
A hair-raising ascent, especially if your car isn't automatic – it's very steep. ⬡ *Map F2*

5 Sacramento up Nob Hill
Take the bus up and hear the engine churning on its painfully slow ascent. ⬡ *Map N3*

6 Noe at 21st Street
At the heights bordering the Castro, Noe Valley, and the Mission, this impossibly steep street will also give you a few chills. ⬡ *Map F5*

7 Potrero Hill
Try Wisconsin Street at 20th for an experience that feels like freefall *(see p109)*.

8 Corona Heights Park
Hiking trails and some spectacular views. ⬡ *Map E4*

9 Russian Hill
One of the best drives in town, with great views of Fisherman's Wharf. ⬡ *Map M2*

10 Filbert Street
There's a sense of flying off into space as you dive over the brink of Hyde and Leavenworth. ⬡ *Map L2*

Left **Greens** Right **Spruce**

Restaurants

1 Quince

Run by Michelin-star chef Michael Tusk, Quince is considered by many to be the best restaurant in the city. It serves dish after dish of beautiful Californian fare, influenced by Northern Italy and made with the freshest local ingredients *(see p91)*.

2 Gitane

Worth a visit as much for its dramatic, gypsy bordello atmosphere as for its delicious Iberian entrées. Drawing on the rich flavours of Portugal, Morocco, southern Spain and France, Gitane offers mouthwatering tagines as well as lamb, pork, and fish dishes, all of which are served with considerable flair *(see p91)*.

3 La Mar

Surprizingly, La Mar is one of San Francisco's few top-notch seafood restaurants. It serves wonderful super-fresh Peruvian seafood (including an astounding assortment of tasty *ceviches*) in a stunning blue and white dining room looking out over the Bay *(see p91)*.

4 A16

Known for its authentic pizzas, fresh pastas, house-cured salami, and regional wines, this casual yet chic marina restaurant will transport you straight to Southern Italy *(see p97)*.

5 Greens

The first fine dining vegetarian restaurant in the city, it was originally inspired by the huge success of the Zen bakery and coffee shop. This spacious, pleasant Marina restaurant came to define vegetarian cuisine for the entire Bay Area *(see p97)*.

6 Delfina

Thanks to its perfect Italian fare made with the freshest local ingredients, it has been hard to get a table at Delfina for years now, which is saying a lot in a city that has trendy restaurants opening every month. In addition to the legendary chicken and delicate pasta dishes at Delfina, you can indulge in the best pizza outside of Italy at its pizzeria next door *(see p113)*.

Delfina

attentiveSan Francisco's Top 10

For a guide to restaurant price ranges **See p91**

Nopalito

From the folks at Nopa *(see p105)* comes a fresh take on Mexican fare. Nopalito focuses on traditional Mexican street food – including carnitas and tacquitos. The cocktails are just as fantastic as the food itself, but be prepared to wait. ⑧ *306 Broderick St. at Oak • Map H3 • (415) 437-0303 • Dis. access • $$*

Ahi Tuna

Spruce

This restaurant's excellent nouveau American menu has a major meat focus. For the same delicious food with a slightly less formal feel, opt to sit in the bar. ⑧ *3640 Sacramento St • Map D3 • (415) 931-5100 • Closed L • Dis. access • $$$$*

Foreign Cinema

In the courtyard, old movies are projected onto a neighboring building while you dine. The food is also excellent and the oyster bar and Sunday brunch are popular. ⑧ *2534 Mission St • Map F5 • (415) 648-7600 • Dis. access • $$$*

Lers Ros Thai

Lers Ros delivers authentic Thai dishes in a no-frills, casual dining room. Arrive early or you'll be standing in line down the street. ⑧ *730 Larkin St • Map K2 • (415) 931-6917 • Dis. access • $*

Top 10 Romantic Dinner Spots

1 Atelier Crenn
Delicious food and the dining room is intimate and quiet. ⑧ *3127 Fillmore • Map E2 • (415) 440-0460 • Dis. access • $$$$*

2 Cliff House
A wild setting with views of crashing waves *(see p115)*.

3 Acquerello
The black truffles are said to be an aphrodisiac. ⑧ *1722 Sacramento St • Map N1 • (415) 567-5432 • $$$$*

4 Masa's Restaurant
French Mediterranean cuisine in elegant surroundings. ⑧ *648 Bush St • Map 4N • (415) 989-7154 • $$$$$*

5 Boulevard
Belle époque decor and extravagant food *(see p113)*.

6 Chez Spencer
The fairy-lit garden complements the French fare. ⑧ *82 14th St • Map G4 • (415) 864-2191 • Dis. access • $$$*

7 Aziza
Delicious, Michelin-star cuisine. ⑧ *5800 Geary Blvd • Map C3 • (415) 752-2222 • Dis. access • $$$*

8 Gary Danko
Sophisticated contemporary cuisine. ⑧ *800 N Point St • Map K2 • (415) 749-2060 • Dis. access • $$$$*

9 Frascati
Italian fare and a great view of the cable car. ⑧ *1901 Hyde St • Map L2 • (415) 928-1406 • Dis. access • $$$*

10 Chez Panisse
The birthplace of Cal-Med cuisine. Book weeks ahead. ⑧ *1517 Shattuck Ave, Berkeley • Hwy 80 • (510) 548-5525 • Dis. access • $$$$$*

Left **Caffè Trieste** Right **Café Flore**

🔟 Cafés

Blue Bottle Café

This hip coffee roaster kicked off San Francisco's latest café trend; Blue Bottle serves up perfect cappuccinos and lattes in its chic industrial SoMa space. Also on offer are Kyoto-style iced-coffees. Perfection takes time, and these barristas take themselves and their work very seriously, so be prepared for a bit of a wait. The experience is worth trying at least once *(see p90)*.

Caffè Trieste

A North Beach landmark that must be experienced if you have any interest whatsoever in this quarter's colorful history – either from the literary and artistic or the Italian points of view. It's a great place for a cup of whatever warm liquid you favor, or to sit and people-watch, or dip into one of the city's free weekly papers *(see p90)*.

Blue Bottle Café

Dolores Park Café

Across the street from historic Mission Dolores, this funky neighborhood café has it all – great views of Dolores Park, filling breakfast and lunch fare, home-made smoothies, freshly baked pastries, and a cool spot to people-watch in the heart of the Mission district. Live music and spoken word performances on Friday nights. 🔊 *501 Dolores St • Map F5 • (415) 621-2936 • Dis. access*

The Grove

This popular spot feels like being at a friend's home with its eclectic mix of furniture and casual vibe. In addition to consistently good coffee, freshly squeezed juices, and healthy breakfast and lunch options are available. The Grove is one of the Marina's best places to go for serious people-watching. 🔊 *2250 Chestnut St between Avila and Scott • Map E2 • (415) 474-4843 • Dis. access*

Brainwash

Café, bar, performance space, and, yes, laundromat, it's got everything the young SoMa loft-dweller could wish for. Fortunately, it's as good a place for eating as it is for washing your clothes or just watching the other customers. The lunch menu features solid international standards such as a great cobb salad, a delicious chicken sandwich, and a range of juicy burgers. 🔊 *1122 Folsom St at 7th • Map R3 • (415) 861-3663 • Dis. access*

Brainwash

Atlas Café
Atlas is as popular for its magazine selection and sunny patio as for its homemade soups and healthy vegan and vegetarian fare. ❀ 3049 20th St at Alabama • Map G5 • (415) 648-1047 • Dis. access

Café Flore
Great for people-watching with outdoor seating and cozy indoor tables, this place is an institution. ❀ 2298 Market St at Noe • Map F5 • (415) 621-8579 • Dis. access

Delessio
Stop by for morning coffee and fresh pastries, or at lunch to sample the extensive buffet and salad bar. ❀ 1695 Market St • Map F4 • (415) 552-5559 • Dis. access

Ritual
Battling Blue Bottle (see p64) to be the coolest coffee shop in the city, Ritual sells and brews its own specialty roasts, sourced from around the world. ❀ 1026 Valencia at 21st • Map F5 • (415) 641-1011 • Dis. access

Papa Toby's Revolution Café and Artbar
Regulars nurse micro-brewed beers or their favorite coffee, and indulge in great pastries. ❀ 3248 22nd St at Bartlett • Map F5 • (415) 642-0474

Top 10 Sunday Brunch Venues

1 Dottie's True Blue Café
The Tenderloin tradition in SoMa – standing in line for the American breakfasts. ❀ 28 6th St • Map G3 • Dis. access • Closed Tue, Wed

2 Sears Fine Food
A Union Square institution, noted for its silver-dollar pancakes (see p91).

3 Ella's
Expect to wait at this breakfast haven. ❀ 500 Presidio Ave • Map E3 • Dis. access

4 Mama's on Washington Square
The greatest French toast in town. ❀ 1701 Stockton St • Map L4 • Dis. access • Closed Mon

5 Sparky's Diner
Hefty omelettes and hash browns draw crowds to this popular 24-hour diner. ❀ 242 Church St at Market • Map F4

6 Presidio Social Club
An elegant restaurant serving up old-school drinks and brunch classics. ❀ 563 Ruger St • Map E2 • Dis. access

7 Just for You
Soul food-inspired brunch in the up-and-coming Dogpatch neighborhood. ❀ 732 22nd St • Map H5 • Dis. access

8 Kate's Kitchen
Huge portions of breakfast specialties, including a "French Toast Orgy". ❀ 471 Haight St • Map F4 • Dis. access

9 Chloe's Café
Banana or pecan pancakes, and cinnamon French toast. ❀ 1399 Church St at 26th • Map F6

10 Red Door Café
As beloved for its comical owner as for its fluffy omelets and perfect French toast. ❀ 1608 Bush St • Map F3

 There are several Bay cruises offering champagne brunches. Telephone Hornblowers (888) 467-6256 for details.

Left **Vesuvio** Right **Americano Bar**

Bars

Bourbon & Branch
You'll need the nightly password to enter this speakeasy bar. Once inside, enjoy the inventive cocktails in one of the most beautifully designed bars in the city, and explore more secret rooms. ⓢ 501 Jones St at O'Farrell • Map P3 • (415) 346-1735

Press Club
A large, modern space just off Market Street, Press Club offers wines from Napa to New Zealand. There are also over 30 beers on tap including some rare selections not often found in the US. Recommended pairings enhance a menu of light bites and entrées (see p90).

Vesuvio
This landmark watering hole was a major Beat and hippie gathering place and attempts to carry on the alternative tradition amid the stained-glass, psychedelic decor. Check out the literary and other memorabilia on

Press Club

the walls and sit on the narrow balcony, from which you can survey the action below. ⓢ 255 Columbus Ave • Map M4 • (415) 362-3370

Americano Bar
The outdoor patio is the big draw at this uber-chic, buzzing bar filled with beautiful people. The views will amaze, as will the drinks and the inviting sleek interior space. Try the plum mojito or a sparkling champagne and the bruschetta with prawns, but beware of the pricey bill. ⓢ 8 Mission St • Map H2 • (415) 278-3777 • Dis. access

Tosca
Ease into the night at this North Beach institution. With Sean Penn and Kid Rock as owners, you can enjoy celebrity-spotting while you sip potent cocktails and listen to opera on the juke box. ⓢ 242 Columbus Ave • Map M4 • (415) 986-9651 • Dis. access

Edinburgh Castle Pub
A hugely happening place incorporating live indie music, a fish 'n' chips delivery service, as well as darts, pool, and general carousing in the Scottish manner. ⓢ 950 Geary St • Map P2 • (415) 885-4074

Lone Palm
A great Mission neighborhood bar with a distinct Casablanca vibe, the Lone Palm

DJ performing at a crowded bar

is known as an ideal spot to sip a scotch and catch up with friends. ✆ 3394 22nd St at Guerrero • Map F5 • (415) 648-0109

Church Key
Boasting the largest beer selection in the city, this is a favorite after-work watering hole and a popular weekend destination. The beer list changes regularly and Church Key offers a variety of fantastic ports and wines as well (see p90).

Blackbird
This super stylish cocktail lounge is swanky enough to draw a cool Castro crowd, but butch enough not to seem like just another gay bar in the neighborhood. The bar draws a big crowd nightly due to its Market Street location, while the craft beers, great selection of Californian wines, and inventive cocktails keep people coming back for more. ✆ 2124 Market St • Map F4 • (415) 503-0630 • Dis. access

Black Horse London Pub
Beloved for its small size, its vast beer selection, and its policy of no cell phones, this tiny little pub is a slice of London life unexpectedly dropped into San Francisco's Marina district. ✆ 1514 Union St at Van Ness • Map L1 • (415) 928-2414

Top 10 San Francisco Tipples

1 Pinot Noir
This full-bodied red is popular for its ability to complement just about any meal. Try Acacia Vineyard.

2 Chardonnay
Of all the whites, this is the most popular, fermented in French oak barrels, lending it smooth vanilla tones. Try Cakebread Cellars.

3 Other Red Wines
Red Zinfandel and Cabernet continue to give Pinot Noir some healthy competition.

4 Other White Wines
Sauvignon Blanc, Chenin Blanc, and Pinot Grigio are the main whites that compete with the Chardonnay grape.

5 Sparkling Wines
Schramsberg's Pinot Noir- and Chardonnay-based sparklers are popular, and there's a lively Prosecco trend sweeping the city.

6 Cocktails
Vintage cocktails like Old Fashioned and Moscow Mule are back in vogue in San Francisco.

7 Beers and Ales
Local breweries abound in the Bay Area, such as Anchor Steam Beer (see p109).

8 Tea
A huge range of infusions, springing from the healthy attitude that dominates here.

9 Coffee
Many more ways to drink your coffee than there are in all of Europe – latte is still the blend of choice.

10 Mineral Water
The top local brand comes and takes its name from Calistoga in the Napa Valley.

Left **The Midnight Sun** Right **Harvey's**

Gay and Lesbian Venues

The Midnight Sun

This popular, posy video bar fills up quickly after office hours and stays that way until the wee hours. Mostly good-looking 20- and 30-somethings, it's more about being admired than making connections here, so it's best to go with a friend or two, have a drink, and then move on to some livelier venue. The videos are a mix of music clips and TV sitcoms. ⊗ *4067 18th St • Map E5 • (415) 861-4186*

Moby Dick

This old-time Castro hangout attracts a more mature crowd. It's generally a bunch of regulars getting together for pinball or pool. The windows are big, so you can keep track of what's going down on the street. The music is largely 1980s retro that sets a fun-loving tone. ⊗ *4049 18th St • Map E5 • (415) 861-1199 • www.mobydicksf.com*

Moby Dick

Twin Peaks

Conveniently located on the corner of Market Street, this legendary and distinctive tavern offers one of the best views of the Castro, whether by day or night. The interior is an inviting, pillowed triangular space with plate-glass windows. ⊗ *401 Castro St • Map E5 • (415) 864-9470*

Eagle SF

Bikers and leather boys still rule at this venerable SoMa dive. Come here to revel in the beer-busting, testosterone-filled atmosphere. The back patio gets going on Sunday afternoons, and Thursdays feature performances by local bands. ⊗ *398 12th St • Map G4*

The Lion Pub

The city's oldest gay bar is also its most upscale. It attracts the more yuppified denizens of the gay community who appreciate the stylish renovated Victorian setting in which it is housed. There's interesting music, a great fireplace, free food at Happy Hour, and hobnobbing with a wealthier clientele. ⊗ *2062 Divisadero St at Sacramento • Map E3 • (415) 567-6565*

Harvey's

Named in honor of the slain gay leader Harvey Milk *(see p39)*, this is the ideal place to get to know the look and feel of the Castro. There's lots of gay

As well as the Castro District, Polk Street (see p85) is also a popular gay area in the city.

The Lion Pub

memorabilia on the walls, the staff are friendly, the ambiance easy-going, and not at all quirky or kinky. It's the wholesome face of gay San Francisco. ⊗ *500 Castro St at 18th • Map E5 • (415) 431-4278*

Martuni's

With its decor of glass and chrome and the regulars' penchant for singing old torch songs, this is a very retro piano bar for an older gay crowd. It's a magnet for butch guys, drag queens, and straights, too – anyone who likes a good sing-along – or who doesn't mind embarassing themselves. ⊗ *4 Valencia St at Market • Map F4 • (415) 241-0205*

Badlands

Its old, dingy interior used to live up to its menacing name, but no more since it has gone all slick and shiny. Still, it's a big draw for the under-40 set. The Sunday afternoon beer bust (4–9pm) is, for many, the most happening event of the week. ⊗ *4121 18th St • Map E5 • (415) 626-9320*

Lush Lounge

It's hard not to have a great time at this lively little piano bar in Polk Gulch. Frequented by the local transvestite community, as well as straight office workers from the surrounding neighborhood, Lush Lounge is always an experience. ⊗ *1221 Polk St at Fern • Map F3 • (415) 771-2022*

Lexington Club

The only full-time "girl" bar in the city, set in a Mission District neighborhood that has been on the rise as a lesbian enclave. Young pierced sylphs, 40-something professionals, and even straight women frequent this fun "down-home, divey den for dykes," as one devotee dubbed it. ⊗ *3464 19th St at Valencia • Map F5 • (415) 863-2052*

The Lexington is one of the few lesbian bars in the city, but all the male gay bars welcome women.

Left **Le Colonial** Right **The Tonga Room**

🔟 Nightlife

1 Le Colonial

People flock here for the cuisine, the live music, or to sit in the lounge for tea or cocktails. Live swing, jazz, and blues bands entertain guests Monday to Thursday, including the very popular Martini Brothers Band. Head to the club upstairs on Friday and Saturday nights as the DJ spins house tracks to a crowded dance floor from 9:30pm–2am. Situated just off Union Square, the location can't be beat *(see p90)*.

2 Mighty

One of the few San Francisco venues large enough to be considered a proper dance club, Mighty is well-known for hip-hop shows and international house DJs. It is beloved by club-goers for its great variety of music, its size, and its revolving art collection *(see p111)*.

Bottom of the Hill

3 Mezzanine

Located in the SoMa district, industrial chic Mezzanine comprises one large room with a long bar down one side, and a concrete dance floor throughout. Mezzanine hosts touring indie bands, esoteric hip-hop acts, and visiting DJs, such as Juan Maclean and the Three 6 Mafia *(see p112)*.

4 Bottom of the Hill

Open seven days a week, this is one of the best live-music venues in a city renowned for its live music. Even though Bottom of the Hill has a definite punk vibe, you are just as likely to hear a folk music act playing as a hardcore punk band. If you don't care for the music, just head to the back where you can grab a table out of earshot *(see p112)*.

5 Harry Denton's Starlight Room

Something for the 40-plus set, or even 50-plus, and those who enjoy good views, cocktails, and dancing. Twenty-two stories above Union Square, couples can dance to jazz and the milder R&B hits, and relax in the easy sophistication of this place. It's 1930s-stylish, so consider it a chance to dress up in suits and party dresses, sip highballs, and enjoy the city's seductive lights. ◈ *Sir Francis Drake Hotel, 450 Powell St at Sutter • Map P4 • (415) 395-8595*

For nightclubs in the Southern neighborhoods see p111

Bimbo's 365 Club

Bimbo's 365 Club
Whether you are into swing, jazz, rock, or grunge, this San Francisco institution delivers. A retro-chic yet unpretentious music venue since 1931, this hopping bar with glittering decor and old-school feel brings in all the top acts. 🅑 *1025 Columbus Ave • Map K3 • (415) 474-0365*

Supperclub
If ultra-chic surroundings are what you are looking for, then this is the club for you – San Francisco at its trendiest. It attracts a young and sexy crowd, and the lighting and music are techno-cool. Whether you are after dancing or highly original performances, this is the place to come. The pricey cover charge is worth it. 🅑 *657 Harrison St • Map Q6 • (415) 348-0900*

Yoshi's
Sushi and jazz may seem like an unusual combination, but once you've set foot inside this San Francisco institution you'll think it a match made in heaven. The restaurant serves delectable sushi while the live music ranges from jazz to pop and world music. 🅑 *1330 Fillmore St • Map E1 • (415) 655-5500*

Punchline Comedy Club
A perfect alternative to bar-hopping, there is no better venue for a good laugh than this hilarious comedy club. National acts (and local ones too) headline a fun evening in an intimate setting, with all the seating up close to the stage. It's best to buy tickets in advance for assured seating. 🅑 *444 Battery St • Map M5 • (415) 397-7573*

The Tonga Room & Hurricane Bar
This Nob Hill tiki bar is almost Disneyesque in its tropical effects, including indoor monsoons and a floating band. Aimed at grown-ups of every age, it delivers kitschy Polynesian dazzlement, and is often chosen as the venue for birthday celebrations. Week-day award-winning Happy Hour (5–7pm) includes an Asian buffet at nominal cost. 🅑 *Fairmont Hotel, 950 Mason St • Map N3 • (415) 772-5278*

Left **Joggers in Golden Gate Park** Right **Surfers**

🔟 Outdoor Activities

Swimming
The icy waters of the Bay are an option only if you're a polar bear or an indomitable surfer. Most visitors will want to head for a pool – try the Embarcadero YMCA. ◈ *Embarcadero YMCA: 169 Steuart St; (415) 957-9622 • Map H2 • www.ymcasf.org*

Hiking
The Bay Area is replete with magnificent hiking trails for every type of nature-lover. Land's End offers some wild terrain to scramble over *(see p117)*, and Mount Tamalpais is criss-crossed with trails *(see p124)*. But just scaling the city's hills is enough hiking for most people.

In-line Skating
Golden Gate Park and in-line skaters make a perfect match, especially on Sundays, when the main street in the park is closed to cars. Or try the path that runs along Marina Green for smoothly paved surfaces.

In-line skater in Golden Gate Park

Skateboarding
Skateboard ramps are wherever you make them in this city – along Market Street in the Financial District, in one of the dozens of parks, or on any plaza. Protection against the inevitable vagaries of flying around on wheels means you should gear up appropriately. ◈ *DLX: 1831 Market St; Map F4 • FTC Skateboarding: 1632 Haight St; Map E4*

Running
Now that Crissy Field's restoration is complete, the Golden Gate Promenade *(see p95)* is an inspiring run. And, of course, Golden Gate Park offers endless opportunities for jogging. If organized running is your thing, try the Bay to Breakers or the San Francisco Marathon. ◈ *Bay to Breakers: 3rd Sun in May; (415) 864-3432; www.baytobreakers.com • San Francisco Marathon: Jun or Jul; (888) 958-6668 • www.runsfm.com*

Tennis
Free public tennis courts abound in the city. Contact the Recreation and Park Department for the one nearest you. Golden Gate Park has courts, for which a small fee is charged, but you can book in advance. Most public outdoor courts are open from sunrise to sunset. Indoor courts are the purview of private tennis clubs, with membership required. ◈ *San Francisco Recreation and Park Department: (415) 831-2700 • Golden Gate Park: (415) 753-7001*

You can rent in-line skates from Skates on Haight, at 1818 Haight Street; tel. (415) 752-8375; www.skatesonhaight.com

Lincoln Park Golf Course

Golf
The Lincoln Park 18-hole course overlooks Land's End, Golden Gate Park has a challenging 9-hole course, and the lovely Presidio Golf Course is considered one of the country's best. *Lincoln Park: (415) 221-9911 • Golden Gate Park: (415) 751-8987 • Presidio Golf Course: (415) 561-4661*

Boating
Sailing, rowing and kayaking are all great here, although far from a cakewalk on the Bay's unpredictable waters and sometimes ferocious prevailing winds. Play it nice and easy by taking a boat out on Stow Lake in Golden Gate Park *(see p21)*.

Extreme Sports
Surfing here requires great fortitude and is not for beginners. The same goes for windsurfing on the Bay. Hang-gliding can be tackled by novices under guidance. *San Francisco Hang-Gliding Center • (510) 528-2300*

Biking
Although the hills' amazing grades overwhelm all but those with legs of steel, bicycling is very big in San Francisco. Don't miss biking across the Golden Gate Bridge. Rent bikes from City Cycle. *City Cycle: 3001 Steiner St • (415) 346-2242 • www.citycycle.com*

Top 10 Spectator Sports

1 SF 49ers
The NFL team plays from September to January. *4900 Marie P. DeBartolo Way, Santa Clara • (415) 656-4900*

2 SF Giants
The city's baseball team plays from April to October. *AT&T Park, 24 Willie Mays Plaza • (415) 972-2000*

3 Golden State Warriors
An NBA basketball team. *Oakland Arena, 7000 Coliseum Way, Oakland • (510) 986-2222*

4 Oakland Athletics
Historic winners of the American Football League in the 1970s. *(510) 638-0500*

5 Oakland Raiders
Members of the American Football League. *(800) 724-3377*

6 Golden Gate Fields
The East Bay venue for horse-racing. *1100 Eastshore Highway, Berkeley • (510) 559-7300*

7 Mazda Raceway Laguna Seca
Grand Prix and motorcycle racing at this 2.2-mile (3.6-km) track. *1021 Monterey-Salinas Hwy, Salinas • (831) 242-8201*

8 Sonoma Raceway
Superbike and auto-racing in the Sonoma Valley. *Hwys 37 & 121, Sonoma • (707) 938-8448*

9 San Jose Sharks
Fast-paced NHL ice hockey. *HP Pavilion, 525 West Santa Clara St, San Jose • 1-800-888-2736*

10 Sacramento Kings
Men's NBA basketball team. *Power Balance Pavilion, 1 Sports Parkway, Sacramento • (916) 928-0000*

Hot-air balloon flights in the Napa Valley, followed by a champagne brunch, are available at www.napavalleyballoons.com

73

Left **Carnaval** Right **St. Patrick's Day Parade**

🔟 Festivals and Parades

St. Patrick's Day Parade
With its large Irish population, not to mention the 25 or so Irish pubs scattered around town, the St. Patrick's Day Parade and the revelry that follows deep into the night is one of the city's largest celebrations. The parade journeys from 2nd and Market streets to the Civic Center.
◉ *Sat or Sun before Mar 17*

Cherry Blossom Festival
Japantown *(see p99)* comes spectacularly to life when the cherry trees blossom. Traditional arts and crafts, *taiko* drumming, martial arts demonstrations, and dancing, as well as delicious Japanese food make this one of the city's favorite celebrations. There's also a colorful and impressive parade. ◉ *Two weekends in Apr*

Cinco de Mayo
Commemorating the defeat of the French army at Puebla, Mexico, in 1862, by General Ignacio Zaragoza, this is one of the Latino community's biggest annual festivals, featuring parades, fireworks, music, and dancing. In addition to the Civic Center, much of the fun happens in the Mission District. ◉ *Sat or Sun before May 5*

Carnaval
Having nothing at all to do with Lent or any other traditional date, San Francisco's Carnaval is staged at the time of year when the weather will most likely be at its best for the glittery event. Groups work all year long, with the help of municipal grants, to create their dazzling costumes and put together their infectiously rhythmic routines, all to a samba, rumba, or salsa beat.
◉ *Mission District • Last weekend in May*

Pride Celebration Parade
More than 300,000 people attend this amazing gay event, the largest of its kind in the US, that takes over Market Street, from the Embarcadero to the Civic Center. It's up to four hours of Dykes on Bikes, drag queens in nuns' habits, leather-clad clones, gay parents, gay marching bands, muscle men, and much more. The floats – as well as the cheering throngs – are likely to be the most over-the-top, outlandish things you've ever witnessed. ◉ *Sun in late Jun*

Performer, Pride Celebration Parade

Chinese New Year

Independence Day
This waterfront festival, held from Aquatic Park to PIER 39, involves live entertainment, food stalls, and state-of-the-art fireworks launched from several points along the Bayfront. If it's foggy, the bursts of light seem that much more romantic. ⊗ Jul 4

Stern Grove Festival
A much loved San Franciscan tradition, this festival showcases every kind of music in an idyllic atmosphere (see p116). ⊗ Sun, early Jun–late Aug

Fleet Week
A celebration of US naval forces, air shows and a parade of ships sail into the bay set against the spectacular San Francisco skyline. ⊗ Oct

Hallowe'en
This boisterous Castro party and parade is a time for dress-up, dress-down, or undress, as the case may be; let your imagination run away with you. ⊗ Oct 31

Chinese New Year
This is the biggest Chinese New Year celebration outside Asia. It incorporates traditional displays and the parade of dragons and performers that winds through Chinatown. ⊗ Jan or Feb

Top 10 Fairs and Gatherings

Haight Street Fair
You'll know hippiedom is alive and well after attending this Gathering of the Tribe. ⊗ Jun

North Beach Festival
The city's oldest street fair features arts and crafts and some great Italian food. ⊗ Jun

Fillmore Street Jazz Festival
Playing up the jazz heritage of this neighborhood, with crafts and live music. ⊗ Early Jul

Folsom Renaissance Faire
This delightful event recreates Elizabethan England, with all its ribaldry and rowdiness. ⊗ Late Aug–early Oct: Sat–Sun

Burning Man
This is group performance art on a behemoth scale in Black Rock Desert, Nevada. ⊗ 1st week Sep

Ghirardelli Square Chocolate Festival
A chocaholic's dream, with the chance to sample various nibbles. ⊗ Early Sep

Folsom Street Fair
One of the biggest events for the gay community is SoMa's leather-and-body-hair carousal. ⊗ Last Sun Sep

Castro Street Fair
A build-up to Hallowe'en, it focuses attention on every-day gay life. ⊗ Early Oct

Tet Festival
A multicultural party, but mainly Vietnamese-American. ⊗ Jan–Feb

Tribal, Folk, & Textile Arts Show
An arts and crafts fair at the Fort Mason Center, offering pottery, jewelry, textiles, and more. ⊗ Early Feb

The best viewing spots for the Independence Day fireworks are Crissy Field or from Telegraph Hill – but expect large crowds.

Left **Baker Beach** Right **Half Moon Bay**

🔟 Beaches

1 Bolinas Beach
This hidden-away Marin beach tends to be windy and is mostly used by dog-walkers, and kayakers. It's sandy, with a backdrop of rocky cliffs. If you walk north, you'll find warmer nooks and crannies out of the wind, where some sun-worshipers bask in the nude, although there is a rarely enforced city ordinance against it (see p124).

2 Stinson Beach
Three miles (5 km) of sand make this one of the most popular beaches in the Bay Area, coupled with the fact that Marin often has fine weather when the rest of the coast is covered in fog. As a result, it can be crowded when the sun comes out (see p124).

3 Muir and Red Rock Beaches
These two beaches, just south of Stinson, are the most famous nude beaches north of San Francisco. Both are sandy curves within their own coves, protected from wind and prying eyes by rocky cliffs. The only caveat is that you'll need sturdy walking shoes to get down the rough paths that lead to them from the parking lots. ⓢ *Muir Beach: off Hwy 1 on Pacific Way • Red Rock: 5.5 miles (9 km) north of Muir on Pacific Way*

4 Baker Beach
This one-mile (1.5-km) stretch of sandy beach, with its perfect views of the Golden Gate Bridge, is the most popular in the city. It's great for sunbathing, dog-walking, picnicking or jogging, but signs warn off swimmers because of riptides. Sunsets here are unforgettable. ⓢ *Map C2*

5 China Beach
Officially called James D. Phelan Beach, this is the poshest beach in San Francisco, being an adjunct to the exclusive Sea Cliff neighborhood. Despite its pedigree, however, California law requires that all coastal areas remain public, although access roads to them can be private. China Beach is small and protected from the wind, there's plenty of parking, and it's a pleasant walk down to the sand. Once there, you'll find showers and even changing rooms. ⓢ *Map B2*

Muir Beach

Note: Swimming is not advisable at many Bay Area beaches because of the cold water and the riptides.

Land's End

Land's End

Although extremely beautiful in a wild, untouched way, this tiny, rocky beach is only for the hardiest nature-lovers. It's quite a hike to get here, although taking the trail up above it is quite a bit easier than going by the lower, coastal trail. Many habitués have built little sun-traps for themselves, by piling up rocks to wall-in their patches of sand *(see p115)*. ✎ Map A3

Ocean Beach

Some 4 miles (6.5 km) long and quite broad, this is the city's largest beach by far, but probably the worst for entering the water safely. It starts at Cliff House and continues on beyond the city limits, turning into picturesque dunes at the southern end. Great for walking or jogging, and when the sun comes out, it's a fine place to sunbathe *(see p115)*.

Half Moon Bay

About 22 miles (35 km) south of the city, the Half Moon Bay shoreline forms a long, gently curving sandy beach accessible at several points off Highway 1. A horseback riding trail runs from Dunes Beach to the bluff area of Francis Beach, and picnicking, kite-flying, surfing, and surf fishing are popular activities. ✎ Hwy 1

San Gregorio Beach

Part of San Gregorio Beach, 11.5 miles (18.5 km) south of Half Moon Bay, is clothing-optional, but it requires a good hike down the cliffs to get to. The entire stretch is partly state park, and includes a protected, driftwood-strewn estuary at the back of a wide, sandy beach, with grassy bluffs along the coast. All along there are protected areas and inlets. The estuary is home to many birds and small animals *(see p127)*.

Pescadero Beach

This beach has a 1-mile (1.5-km) shoreline with sandy coves, rocky cliffs, tide pools, surf-fishing spots, and picnic facilities. Across the highway is Pescadero Marsh Natural Preserve, a popular area for bird-watchers and other naturalists, being a refuge for blue heron, kites, deer, raccoons, foxes and skunks. The beach is 14.5 miles (23.3 km) south of Half Moon Bay on Highway 1 *(see p127)*.

Left **Coastal beach** Right **Monterey harbor**

🏆10 Day Trips from the City

1 Wine Country

Taking at least a day to drive up into the Napa-Sonoma hill country should be on everyone's list. Not only is the countryside beautiful, but you can also sample some of the best wines in the world. Dip into the restorative volcanic hot springs, and enjoy lavish spa treatments *(see pp32–5)*.

California wine

2 Muir Woods

At the foot of Mount Tamalpais *(see p124)*, this 550-acre woodland is home to one of the few remaining first-growth groves of redwoods. The oldest of these giants is at least 1,000 years old, and such trees once covered the coastal area of California. The woods are named in honor of John Muir, the 19th-century conservationist *(see p39)*. 🔆 Muir Woods National Monument • Open 8am–sunset daily • Adm • (415) 388-2595 • www.nps.gov/muwo/

Muir Woods

3 Monterey

This town is renowned for its world-class aquarium, the Monterey Jazz and Blues Festivals, and Cannery Row, made famous by the author John Steinbeck, who described it in many of his famous books. Established by the Spanish in 1770, Monterey was the first capital of California *(see p36)* – some early buildings survive. 🔆 Monterey Bay Aquarium • Open 10am–6pm daily (9:30am–6pm in summer) • (831) 648-4800 • Dis. access • Adm • www.mbayaq.org

4 Big Basin State Park, Boulder Creek

Highway 9 is one of the most picturesque drives in the Bay Area, winding its way among the green Santa Cruz Mountains and through little towns. Although it's minutes from Silicon Valley, life has a backwoods feel here.

5 Stanford University

Just 30 minutes south of the city, with a CalTrain depot right at the main gates, the palm-lined beauties of this campus make it worth a trip. The visual motif of sandstone and red-tile roofs has been carried forward since the Romanesque Quadrangle was built in the late 1800s. The ornate carvings that decorate the arches and pillars are extraordinarily lovely, setting off the elaborate mosaic that graces the façade of Memorial Church *(see p125)*.

The Oceanic Society conducts expeditions to the annual gray whale migration. Contact (415) 474-3385 for details.

Carmel-by-the-Sea

Carmel-by-the-Sea was founded as an artists' colony in the early 1900s, and is now one of the most exclusive communities in the world – having boasted actor Clint Eastwood as its mayor in 1986–88. Its old Spanish mission, one of the 21 built along the coast (see p30) is considered California's most beautiful. ◈ Carmel Mission: 3080 Rio Rd • Open 9:30am–5pm Mon–Sat; 10:30am–5pm Sun • (831) 624-1271 • Adm • www.carmelmission.org

Coastal Beaches

At least 20 different beaches line Highway 1 south of San Francisco. Some of these include Gray Whale Cove, Montara State Beach, Miramar Beach and El Granada Beach, Roosevelt Beach, Dunes Beach, Francis Beach, Poplar Beach, Pelican Point Beach, Cowell Ranch State Beach, Martin's Beach, San Gregorio Beach, Pescadero State Beach, Bean Hollow State Beach, and Pebble Beach.

Point Reyes

Some 110 sq miles (285 sq km) of pristine natural coastline make this promontory a haven for all sorts of wildlife and a thing of unforgettable, wind-swept beauty. You can watch whales and sea lions from Point Reyes Lighthouse (see p127).

Santa Cruz

This beach resort has always had a reputation for the vibrancy of its countercultural way of life. Along the beautiful coastline, the most prominent feature is the Boardwalk's Big Dipper Roller-coaster, which has been thrilling Santa Cruzers since 1923. The best swimming in the Bay Area is also here (see p127).

Carmel Mission

Saratoga and Los Gatos

Both of these towns, in the hills above Silicon Valley, have retained their frontier quality. One of the best things to do, other than drive the scenic roads, is to visit Hakone Gardens, a beautiful Japanese park (see p127). ◈ Hakone Gardens: 21000 Big Basin Way, Saratoga • (408) 741-4994 • Open 10am–5pm Mon–Fri, 11am–5pm Sat–Sun • Adm • www.hakone.com

AROUND TOWN

SAN FRANCISCO'S TOP 10

Left **Bank of California, Financial District** Right **City Hall, Civic Center**

Downtown

THE DOWNTOWN AREA IS SMALL BUT HIGHLY VARIEGATED, *including some of the city's oldest and newest landmarks, as well as some of its most exotic and eccentric neighborhoods. Colorful Chinatown, exuberant*

North Beach, posh Nob and Russian Hills, the bustling Financial District, the graceful Ferry Building, and the noble architecture and cultural venues of the Civic Center – all these and more are packed into San Francisco's heart. This is where you can ride the legendary cable cars on their most scenic routes (see pp10–11), and don't forget to climb up Telegraph Hill, where Coit Tower stands as one of the city's most loved landmarks, competing successfully with the Transamerica Pyramid not far away.

Chinatown

🔟 Sights

1. Chinatown
2. Grace Cathedral
3. North Beach
4. Nob Hill
5. Russian Hill
6. Jackson Square
7. Civic Center
8. Union Square
9. Financial District
10. Exploratorium

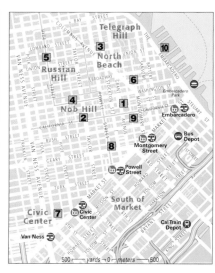

Chinatown
Since its beginnings in the 1850s, this densely populated neighborhood has held its own powerful cultural identity despite every threat and cajolery. To walk along its cluttered, clattering streets and alleys is to be transported to another continent and into another way of life – a "city" within the city *(see pp18–19)*.

Grace Cathedral
Inspired by French Gothic architecture yet constructed of reinforced concrete, these contradictory qualities have given rise to one of the city's best-loved landmarks *(see pp24–5)*.

North Beach
This lively neighborhood is the city's original "Little Italy" and is still noted for its great Italian restaurants and cafés, mostly lined up along and near Columbus Avenue. In the 1950s, it was also a magnet for the Beat writers and poets, notably Jack Kerouac and Allen Ginsberg *(see pp52–3)*, who brought to the area a Bohemian style which it still sports today. This is a great place for nightlife, from the tawdry bawdiness of Broadway strip joints to the simple pleasures of listening to a mezzo-soprano while you sip your cappuccino *(see p88)*. ◈ *Map L4*

Nob Hill
With the advent of the cable car, San Francisco's highest hill was quickly peopled with the elaborate mansions of local magnates – in particular, the "Big Four" who built the Transcontinental railway *(see p39)* – and the

Nob Hill

name has become synonymous with wealth and power. The 1906 earthquake, however, left only one "palace" standing, now the Pacific Union Club, which still proudly dominates the center of the summit. Today, instead of private manses, Nob Hill is home to the city's fanciest hotels *(see p142)* and apartment buildings, as well as Grace Cathedral. ◈ *Map N3*

Russian Hill
Another of San Francisco's precipitous heights, one side of which is so steep you'll find no street at all, only steps. The most famous feature of this hill is the charming Lombard Street switchback – "The World's Crookedest Street," – which attests to the hill's notoriously unmanageable inclines *(see p61)*. As with Nob Hill, with the cable car's advent, Russian Hill was claimed by the wealthy, and it maintains a lofty position in San Francisco society to this day. It supposedly took its name from the burial place of Russian fur traders, who were among the first Europeans to ply their trade at this port in the early 1800s. ◈ *Map M2*

Benjamin Franklin statue,
North Beach

The Making of a City

The Bay lay undiscovered by Europeans until 1769, and for years was little more than a Spanish mission village called Yerba Buena, becoming Mexican in 1821. The first great boost came when gold was discovered at Sutter's Mill in 1848. Hundreds of thousands from all over the world came to try their luck in the Gold Rush. At the same time, the US took possession of the West Coast. The Transcontinental Railway helped to firmly establish the area's financial base.

Jackson Square

Renovated in the 1950s, this neighborhood right next to the Transamerica Pyramid *(see p46)* contains some of San Francisco's oldest buildings. In the 19th century the area was notorious for its squalor, and was nick-named the "Barbary Coast," but brothels and drinking establishments have given way today to upscale offices and the city's most lavish antiques shops. The blocks around Jackson Street and Hotaling Place feature many original brick, cast-iron, and granite façades. Map M5

Jackson Square

Civic Center

The city's administrative center is an excellent example of grand Beaux Arts taste and illustrates San Franciscans' pride in their city *(see p46)*. It is perhaps the most ambitious and elaborate city center complex in the US and it continues to undergo enhancements. Besides the imposing City Hall, with its vast rotunda, gold-leaf detailing, and formal gardens, the area also includes the War Memorial Opera House, the Louise M. Davies Symphony Hall, the Herbst Theater *(see p56)*, the State Building, the New Main Library, and the monumental Old Main Library, re-inaugurated as the Asian Art Museum. Map R1

Union Square

This important square, which gets its name from the pro-Union rallies held here in the early 1860s, has a $25-million upgraded look that includes performance spaces, grassy terraces, and improved parking. It is now the center for high-end shopping. Located with the edges of the Financial District on one side and the Theater District on the other *(see pp50–51)*, it is at its most picturesque along Powell Street, where the cable cars pass right in front of the historic St Francis Hotel *(see p143)*. The column in the center commemorates Admiral Dewey's victory at Manila Bay during the Spanish-American War of 1898. Map P4

Financial District

Montgomery Street, now the heart of the Financial District, was once lined with small shops where miners came to weigh their gold dust. It marks roughly

There are walking tours of the Financial District run by Hobnob Tours; call (650) 814 6303 or visit www.hobnobtours.com

First Interstate Center, Financial District

the old shoreline of shallow Yerba Buena Cove, which was filled in during the Gold Rush to create more land. Today it is lined with early 20th-century banking "temples" and modern fabrications of glass and steel. At the end of Market Street stands the renovated Ferry Building, which once handled 100,000 commuters a day before the city's bridges were constructed, and is now a bustling meeting spot with cafés and artisan food shops. Its tower is inspired by the Moorish belfry of Seville Cathedral in Spain. ◈ *Map M5*

Exploratorium

One of the world's first hands-on science museums, the Exploratorium now stands in a spectacular location on Pier 15. There are close to 600 exhibits that are spread among themed indoor galleries and a large outside space. There are also educational programs, a theater, an interactive gift shop, a Bay Observatory, an outdoor plaza, and cafés *(see p58)*. ◈ *Pier 15, Embarcadero • Map L6 • (415) 563-7337*
• *See website for opening hours*
• *Adm • www.exploratorium.edu*

A Walk Around North Beach

Morning

Start at the top of North Beach, on **Telegraph Hill** *(see p88)*, admire the famous views, and visit **Coit Tower** *(see p46)*, making sure to take in the murals. Next, walk down to **Filbert Street** *(see p88)* and go right a couple of blocks until you get to lovely **Washington Square**, where, at **Saints Peter and Paul Catholic Church**, Marilyn Monroe and local baseball great Joe DiMaggio had their wedding pictures taken *(see p88)*. Continue on along Columbus Avenue to the left and pay a visit at colorful **Caffè Roma** *(see p90)*, where you can indulge in a bit of sidewalk ogling. Or, across the street, pay homage to the time-honored **US Restaurant** *(see p91)* which serves some of the best pasta in town.

Afternoon

After lunch, take a left on Green Street and go over one block to **Upper Grant** *(see p88)*, with its funky shops and bars, a regular hangout since the 1950s. Turn right on to Vallejo Street, where a visit to the famous **Caffè Trieste** *(see p90)* for a coffee and the authentic Bohemian atmosphere is a must. Continue on down Columbus to William Saroyan Place and at No. 12 you'll find Specs', an exuberant bar filled with Beat memorabilia. Finally, just across Columbus at No. 261 is the immortal **City Lights Bookstore** *(see p88)*, where you can browse the Beat poetry written by owner Lawrence Ferlinghetti and friends.

Left **City Lights Bookstore** Right **Filbert Street Steps**

TOP 10 North Beach Sights

Telegraph Hill
Named after the semaphore installed on its crest in 1850, the hill's eastern side was dynamited to provide rocks for landfill. Steps descend its slopes, lined with gardens. At its summit stands Coit Tower. ◈ *Map L5*

North Beach Views
The panoramic views from both the hill and the top of the Coit Tower are justly celebrated. The wide arc sweeping from the East Bay and the Bay Bridge to Alcatraz and the Golden Gate Bridge is breathtaking.

Coit Tower Murals
The frescoes were painted by local artists in 1934, to provide jobs during the Depression *(see p47)*. The murals are socio-political commentary yet are also appealing for their details of life in California at the time. ◈ *Map L5*

Filbert Street Steps
The flowery descent down these rustic steps provides great views of the Bay. ◈ *Map L5*

City Lights Bookstore
The Beat poet Lawrence Ferlinghetti founded City Lights in 1953. It's a great place to leaf through a few volumes of poetry or the latest free papers to find out what's on.
◈ *261 Columbus Ave*
• Map M4 • (415) 362-8193

Broadway
Made famous in the 1960s for its various adult entertainments, the offerings haven't changed much, though today many venues are now more mainstream. ◈ *Map M5*

Upper Grant
Saloons, cafés, and bluesy music haunts give this northerly section of Grant Avenue a very alternative feel. ◈ *Map L4*

Caffè Trieste
If you're in the neighborhood on a Saturday afternoon, don't miss the spirited opera that takes place here, one of the longest-running informal musical shows in the city *(see p90)*.

Washington Square
This pretty park is lined with Italian bakeries, restaurants and bars. Don't be surprised to see practitioners of *t'ai chi* doing their thing on the lawn every morning. ◈ *Map L4*

Saints Peter & Paul Church
Neo-Gothic in conception, with an Italianesque façade, this church is also called the Italian Cathedral and the Fisherman's Church, since many Italians who originally lived in the neighborhood made their living by fishing *(see p45)*.
◈ *666 Filbert St • Map L4*
• Open daily • Free

Coit Tower

Around Town – Downtown

There are guided tours of North Beach's Italian and Beat history, food and culture. Contact the tourist office (see p132) for details.

Left **Serge Sorokko Gallery** Right **W. Graham Arader III**

🔟 Downtown Shopping

Shreve & Co
A San Francisco original and one of the city's most elegant jewelers. In addition to gems set in wonderful ways, you'll also find fine timepieces, Limoges porcelain, and Lalique crystal.
🚫 *200 Post St at Grant • Map P4 • (415) 421-2600 • Dis. access*

W. Graham Arader III
One of Jackson Square's most appealing shops is like an art museum, featuring fine antique prints. You can marvel at Audubon's *Birds of America*, ancient maps, and historic prints.
🚫 *435 Jackson St, Jackson Square • Map M5 • (415) 788-5115 • Dis. access*

Carrots
A beautiful women's clothing boutique located in a charming brick building near Jackson Square. 🚫 *843 Montgomery St • Map M5 • (415) 834-9040 • Dis. access*

Little Vine
Grab one of the sandwich specials while browsing this quaint, European-inspired shop, filled with independently produced wines, artisan cheeses, pickles, and locally-sourced honey. 🚫 *1541 Grant Ave • Map P4 • (415) 738-2221*

Serge Sorokko Gallery
If you're in the market for something by one of the modern masters, this is an excellent place to browse. Important prints and other works by Picasso, Matisse, Mirò, Chagall, and other 20th-century greats, such as Tapiès, Bacon, Twombly, and Warhol. 🚫 *55 Geary St • Map P4 • (415) 421-7770*

Christopher-Clark Fine Art
Another gallery for modern European and American masters. A good stock of Bay Area artists, too. 🚫 *377 Geary Blvd • Map P4 • (415) 397-7781 • Dis. access*

Schein & Schein
Antique maps and prints, fine engravings, rare books, and unique items fill this quaint shop. Owner Jimmie Schein is a rich source of local history. 🚫 *1435 Grant Ave • Map G2 • (415) 399-8882*

The North Face
Another San Francisco original, you'll find everything for the outdoor adventurer at this popular chain. 🚫 *180 Post St • Map P4 • (415) 433-3223 • Dis. access*

Macchiarini Creative Design
The oldest ongoing metal arts design house, production studio, and gallery in the US hand-crafting individually made sculptures and jewelry. 🚫 *1544 Grant Ave • Map G2 • (415) 982-2229*

William Stout Architectural Books
A landmark for design buffs the world over, this small space is divided in two, with newer books upstairs. 🚫 *804 Montgomery St • Map M4 • (415) 391-6757*

Left **Press Club** Right **Tosca**

TOP 10 Cafés and Bars

1 Caffè Trieste
One of the most authentic cafés in town, rich with arty non-chalance (see p64). ◈ 609 Vallejo St • Map M4 • (415) 982-2605 • Dis. access

2 Tosca
Dating back to 1919, this North Beach bar is a favorite with celebrities. The jukebox plays opera arias. ◈ 242 Columbus Ave • Map M4 • Closed L • (415) 986-9651 • Dis. access

3 Caffè Roma
You're as likely to hear Italian here as you are English. Caffè Roma offers a friendly atmosphere in which to enjoy an espresso and eye passers-by. ◈ 526 Columbus Ave • Map L4 • (415) 296-7942 • Dis. access

4 Blue Bottle Café
A cool modern space known for its hip crowd, and for turning out some of the city's best coffees (see p64). ◈ 66 Mint St • Map Q4 • (510) 653-3394 • Dis. access

5 Café de la Presse
This small corner café carries an impressive assortment of international newspapers, and style and design magazines. Grab a table and just watch the world go by. ◈ 352 Grant Ave at Sutter • Map N5 • (415) 398-2680

6 Royal Exchange
For a proper beer and burger, head to this classic watering hole, which has more than 30 beers on tap. ◈ 301 Sacramento St • Map N6 • (415) 956-1710 • Dis. access

7 Le Colonial
Sit back and unwind with a cocktail among the tropical plants at this Vietnamese restaurant. Happy hour is from 5 to 6:30pm daily (see p70). ◈ 20 Cosmo Place • Map N3 • (415) 931-3600

8 Church Key
This Victorian-themed bar has one of the city's largest beer selections (see p67). ◈ 1402 Grant Ave at Green St • Map L4 • (415) 963-1713

9 Bix
Tucked into a Downtown alley, this sultry supper club features potent cocktails and smooth jazz. ◈ 56 Gold St between Montgomery and Sansome • Map M5 • (415) 433-6300

10 Press Club
This popular ultra-modern wine lounge offers a wide selection of wines and a specially crafted menu to accompany them (see p66). ◈ 20 Yerba Buena Ln at Market • Map P4 • (415) 744-5000

Price Categories

For a three-course meal for one with half a bottle of wine (or equivalent meal), taxes and extra charges.

$	under $20
$$	$20–$40
$$$	$40–$55
$$$$	$55–$80
$$$$$	over $80

Above **Yank Sing**

₁₀ Places to Eat

1 Quince
The Northern Italian cuisine made with local ingredients has earned rave reviews at this Michelin-star restaurant *(see p62).* ☎ *470 Pacific Ave • Map M5 • (415) 775-8500 • Closed L • Dis. access • $$$$*

2 Kokkari Estiatorio
The Greek cuisine here is a delectable revelation of flavors. The lamb shank and grilled octopus are not to be missed. ☎ *200 Jackson St • Map M6 • (415) 981-0983 • $$$$*

3 La Mar
Innovative Peruvian seafood restaurant situated on the waterfront *(see p62).* ☎ *Pier 1.5 Embarcadero at Washington • Map M6 • (415) 397-8880 • Closed L • $$$*

4 One Market
The views of the Bay's lights are spectacular at night, and the farm-fresh food memorable. ☎ *1 Market St at Steuart • Map N6 • (415) 777-5577 • Closed Sun • Dis. access • $$$$*

5 Slanted Door
This Vietnamese favorite serves tantalizing dishes. ☎ *1 Ferry Building • Map H2 • (415) 861-8032 • Dis. access • $$$*

6 Gitane
Gypsy chic meets classic Iberian cuisine at this popular restaurant, located on a charming cobbled alley *(see p62).* ☎ *6 Claude Lane at Sutter • Map P4 • (415) 788-6686 • Closed L • Dis. access • $$$*

7 Sotto Mare
This lively restaurant consistently turns out terrific Italian seafood dishes. Be prepared for a wait. ☎ *552 Green St • Map L4 • (415) 398-3181 • $$*

8 Sears Fine Food
This 1950s retro coffee shop is famous for its breakfasts, and is always good for a quick fill-up *(see p65).* ☎ *439 Powell St • Map P4 • (415) 986-0700/1160 • Dis. access • $*

9 Tadich Grill
A favorite since 1849, Tadich serves classics such as clam chowder. Brusque staff add some fun to the atmosphere. ☎ *240 California St • Map N5 • (415) 391-1849 • Dis. access • $$$*

10 Yank Sing
Yank Sing is famous for its signature Shanghai dumplings, with over 60 varieties on offer. Weekday lunchtimes can be crowded. ☎ *101 Spear St • Map H2 • (415) 957-9300 • Dis. access • $$$*

Note: Unless otherwise stated, all restaurants accept credit cards and serve vegetarian meals

91

Left **Logo, Fort Mason Center** Right **Hyde Street Pier, The Embarcadero**

The North Shoreline

AS ITS NAME SUGGESTS, the Bayshore area spreads out along the Bay at San Francisco's northern edge. This impressive shoreline faces the islands and enjoys unforgettable views of both the Bay and Golden Gate Bridges. Historically, the city began its life here, when the Spanish set up a military outpost at the Presidio in 1776. More history can be found at the piers of the northern Embarcadero, including now heavily commercialized PIER 39 and Fisherman's Wharf, where San Francisco's fishing industry began in the 19th century. But also part of the area is the smart Marina District, with its swanky homes and two yacht clubs. Some of the finest parks are found here too, most notably the Presidio, Crissy Field, the Marina Green, and the Great Meadow above the Fort Mason Center. The area is also home to the particularly stylish and sole-surviving remnant of the 1915 Panama-Pacific Exposition – the Neo-Classical Palace of Fine Arts.

🔟 Sights

1. Golden Gate Bridge
2. Fisherman's Wharf
3. Alcatraz
4. Angel, Treasure, and Yerba Buena Islands
5. The Embarcadero
6. Fort Mason Center
7. Marina District
8. Palace of Fine Arts
9. Crissy Field
10. The Presidio

Ferry Building, Embarcadero

Golden Gate Bridge

Golden Gate Bridge
This world-famous engineering masterpiece sets off the entrance to San Francisco Bay in the most spectacular way, and never fails to elicit gasps of awe from first-time visitors and old-timers alike *(see pp8–9).*

Fisherman's Wharf
Although now largely tourist-oriented, there are still authentic sights to see, aromas to savor, and salt air to breathe among these piers *(see pp12–13).*

Alcatraz
America's "Devil's Island" didn't operate as a prison for very long, but the cell blocks and control room can still evoke a chill *(see pp14–17).*

Angel, Treasure, and Yerba Buena Islands
A trip out to Angel Island, now a state park, can make for a very pleasant day of picnicking, biking, hiking, kayaking, and swimming. But in the early 1900s it was the "Ellis Island of the West," where would-be immigrants, mostly Chinese, could be detained for months. During World War II, it served as a prisoner of war camp and later as a missile base. Treasure Island was built in 1939 for the Golden Gate International Exposition and was a US Navy base during World War II; it is now once again owned by the city and has become one of San Francisco's suburbs. Yerba Buena Island is a Coast Guard station and is mostly closed to visitors.
⊗ *Ferries from Pier 41*

The Embarcadero
The Embarcadero starts at Aquatic Park and curves all the way around to Hunters Point at the southeastern edge of the city. Since the Port of Oakland handles the Bay's shipping needs, the old piers are used for any number of purposes these days, and the parallel road has become a park promenade *(see p49).* PIER 39 is the most famous since it was turned into an amusement attraction in the 1980s, while other piers house concerts, festivals, antiques fairs, and restaurants. When looking for a particular pier, note that those to the north of the Ferry Building have odd numbers and those to the south, even.
⊗ *Map G1*

Sea lions on PIER 39, Fisherman's Wharf

View of the Marina District

Fort Mason Center

Formerly a military base established during the Civil War, some of the army buildings have been devoted to cultural programs of all kinds since 1976. Some 50 organizations now call it home, including museums, art galleries, theaters, shops, festivals, fairs, and performance spaces, as well as libraries and various institutes. Some of the most prominent are The Mexican Museum and the Museo ItaloAmericano (see p42), the Long Now Museum, SFMOMA Artists Gallery, the Children's Art Center, the Magic Theater (see p57), and Herbst Pavilion. The city's finest vegetarian restaurant, Greens, is also located here, enjoying unique views of the Bay and Golden Gate (see p97). Map F1

Marina District

This is a pleasant, upmarket zone, featuring bars and trendy boutiques along Chestnut Street. Marina Green is a vast lawn where locals love to jog, skate, fly kites, picnic, or walk their dogs. At the tip of the break-water that protects the Marina, you can tune in to the bizarre sounds of the Wave Organ, an instrumental structure of underwater pipes through which the tides slosh in a vaguely musical fashion. Map E1

Palace of Fine Arts

The sole survivor – with a lot of help from restorers – of the many fantasy monuments built for the 1915 Panama-Pacific Exposition, the Neo-Classical Palace was an Expo' center-piece. The dome of the rotunda is supported by a classical frieze and an octagonal arcade, which is set off by a landscaped lagoon and flanked by an open peristyle of Corinthian columns (see p46). The palace was rebuilt in 1965 and now houses the Palace of Fine Arts Theatre, a venue that successfully entertains a wide range of audiences. Events include lectures, comedy, and dance. Many people also go to the palace to enjoy the grounds. 3301 Lyon St • Map E1 • Box office: (415) 567-6642; general info: (415) 563-6504 • See website for event times • Adm • www.palaceoffinearts.org

Crissy Field

Originally marshland and dunes, the field was filled in for the 1915 Pan-Pacific Exposition and paved over entirely for use as an airfield by the army from 1919–36. With the establishment of the Presidio as a national park

For information on the full range of events offered at the Fort Mason Center during your visit, go to www.fortmason.org

under the supervision of the city, a massive restoration project has now returned part of Crissy Field to wetlands and the rest to lawns, pathways, and picnic areas. The city's 100-acre "Front Yard" is one of the prime viewing sites for the July 4 fireworks displays, while the Golden Gate Promenade is a 3-mile (5-km) paved pathway that runs through this district from Aquatic Park to Fort Point. ◈ Map D1

10 The Presidio

This beautiful wooded corner of the city has stunning views over the Golden Gate, but from 1776 until 1994 it was owned and occupied by first the Spanish, then the Mexican, and finally, the US armies, and almost entirely off-limits to anyone else. It is now a major part of the Golden Gate National Recreational Area. It is a spectacular park, full of nature trails, streams, forests, drives, and historic structures. In 2005 filmmaker George Lucas installed his production company, LucasFilm, here, creating a \$350-million headquarters. Also here is the Walt Disney Family Museum, which provides insight into the life of Walt Disney through photographs, animation, and an impressive range of interactive exhibits *(see p48)*. ◈ Map D2

Presidio Officers' Club, The Presidio

A Bike Ride through the Presidio

🕐 Beginning at the Visitor Information Center, where you can pick up an excellent map, first explore the Main Post. Here you can ride around the Parade Ground, see the Presidio's earliest surviving buildings, dating from the 1860s, as well as 18th-century Spanish adobe wall fragments in the former Officers' Club.

Exit the area on Sheridan, which takes you past the Spanish Colonial Revival-style Golden Gate Club, and turn left onto Lincoln, which winds around the National Military Cemetery. Turn right on McDowell; on the left you see the Colonial Revival Cavalry Barracks.

Now go past the five brick Stables, off to both the left and the right, and stop at the quirky Pet Cemetery on the left, where post guard dogs are buried as well as many other family pets. Next, head under Highway 101 to encounter Stilwell Hall, built in 1921 as enlisted barracks and a mess hall for the airmen; turn left to take in the metal Aerodrome Hangars from the same era; then proceed on and pause at **Crissy Field** to admire the views.

Double back at this point to take the next left down toward the Bay itself and join the Golden Gate Promenade all the way out to Fort Point. As long as the fog is not too bad, this is the perfect spot to experience the awe-inspiring **Golden Gate Bridge** *(see pp8–9)* and the crashing waves of the mighty Pacific.

For bike rentals **See p134.** The Presidio visitor center is temporarily located at 105 Montgomery St on the Main Post.

95

Left **Ghirardelli chocolate bars** Right **Cost Plus World Market**

☒10 Wharf Area Shops

Ghirardelli Chocolate
Stop by for a free sample and then stock up on your mouth-watering favorites. If you're feeling nostalgic take home some chocolate cable cars. ◊ *Ghirardelli Square, 900 North Point St • Map K2 • (415) 775-5500*

Gigi & Rose
Whimsical gifts, candy, and clothes adorn this lovely shop with one-of-a-kind accessories, children's outfits and shoes all designed by the owners. ◊ *Ghirardelli Square, 900 North Point St • Map K2 • (415) 765-9060*

One of a Kind
This aptly named boutique features unique, beautifully crafted wooden pieces, including jewelry boxes, bowls, hand-carved animals, and coffee tables. ◊ *Ghirardelli Square, 900 North Point St • Map K2 • (415) 776-3200*

Lola of North Beach
Don't miss the wonderful souvenir section, stationery, and locally-designed glassware and ornaments at this quaint gift shop. ◊ *Ghirardelli Square, 900 North Point St • Map K2 • (415) 567-7760*

Jackson & Polk
A little bit of everything is offered in this boutique of books and treasures, which prides itself on offering a wide selection of San Francisco-based brands. ◊ *Ghirardelli Square, 900 North Point • Map K2 • (415) 345-9708*

N.F.L. Shop
Officially licensed to sell products for all major league sports, so here's your chance to stock up on the jerseys and caps of all your favorite teams. ◊ *PIER 39, Ground Level • Map J4 • (415) 397-2027*

Patagonia
The San Francisco store of this quintessentially Californian company sells classic fleeces and outdoor wear, all guaranteed to last forever. One percent of annual sales are donated to environmental charities. ◊ *700 North Point St • Map J4 • (415) 771-2050*

elizabethW
This boutique offers delightful fragrances, soaps, lotions, sachets, and scented candles all made locally. ◊ *Ghirardelli Square, 900 North Point St • Map K2 • (415) 441-8354*

Cost Plus World Market
The original world import mart that set the trend for all the others. It can still surprise with a well-chosen item from some far-away land. ◊ *2552 Taylor St • Map K3 • (415) 928-6200*

Reader's Bookstore
Great secondhand books, records, and CDs, and all the proceeds support programs in San Francisco's libraries. No better prices anywhere. ◊ *Fort Mason Center, Building C • Map F1 • (415) 771-1076*

Price Categories

For a three-course meal for one with half a bottle of wine (or equivalent meal), taxes and extra charges.

$	under $20
$$	$20–$40
$$$	$40–$55
$$$$	$55–$80
$$$$$	over $80

Above **Scoma's**

🔟 Places to Eat

Gary Danko
The French-American menu allows you to create your own mix 'n' match fixed-price selection. If you don't have a reservation, head for the bar, where you can order anything on the menu. ❧ *800 North Point St at Hyde • Map K2 • (415) 749-2060 • Dis. access • $$$$$*

The Codmother
This food truck serves outstanding fish tacos, fish and chips, and assorted chip shop desserts, like fried Oreos. ❧ *2824 Jones St • Map J4 • (415) 606-9349 • Closed D • Dis. access • $*

Tacolicious
A multitude of taco choices abound at this popular joint. Enjoy the free chips and salsa while you wait. ❧ *2301 Chestnut St • Map K4 • (415) 346-1966 • $$*

Isa
At this tiny Marina discovery the concept is nouvelle French tapas, such as honey-spiced calamari, and lobster broth sprinkled with tarragon. ❧ *3324 Steiner St between Chestnut and Lombard • Map E2 • (415) 567-9588 • Dis. access • $$$*

A16
An authentic southern Italian dining experience that's worth dressing up for *(see p62).* ❧ *2355 Chestnut St • Map E1 • (415) 771-2216 • Dis. access • $$$$*

Greens
Two decades of inventive vegetarian dishes plus panoramas add up to a treat *(see p62).* ❧ *Fort Mason Center, Buchanan St, Building A • Map F1 • (415) 771-6222 • Dis. access • $$$*

Zarzuela
Delicious, well-priced tapas is served up in this cozy restaurant. ❧ *2000 Hyde St • Map L2 • (415) 346-0800 • Dis. access • $$$*

Scoma's
A Fisherman's Wharf seafood tradition since 1965 *(see p12).* Enjoy the cracked crab roasted in garlic and olive oil. ❧ *Pier 47 on A1 Scoma Way • Map J2 • (415) 771-4383 • Dis. access • $$*

Zushi Puzzle
One of the best sushi spots in the city, thanks to its super-fresh fish and friendly chef. ❧ *1910 Lombard St • Map F2 • (415) 931-9319 • Closed L • $$$*

The Buena Vista Café
This café claims to have invented Irish coffee. The menu features classic American dishes. ❧ *2765 Hyde St • Map K2 • (415) 474-5044 • Dis. access • $$*

Note: *Unless otherwise stated, all restaurants accept credit cards and serve vegetarian meals*

Left **Union Street** Right **Golden Gate Park**

Central Neighborhoods

AS WITH EVERY QUADRANT OF SAN FRANCISCO, *diversity is the keynote here. This area encompasses the oldest money and the highest society of the city's founding families, as well as some of the poorest of citizens. It takes in the staunchest pillars of the politically savvy – though true conservatives are a rarity in this progressive city – as well as the wildest let-it-all-hang-out free-thinkers. Then, too, there's a considerable swathe of the comfortably middle-class who, like all San Franciscans, are simply intent on enjoying the beauties and pleasures of their great city.*

Spreckels Mansion

🔟 Sights and Neighborhoods

1. Golden Gate Park
2. Union Street
3. Pacific Heights
4. Japantown
5. Haight-Ashbury
6. Hayes Valley
7. Geary Boulevard
8. Presidio Heights
9. Western Addition
10. The Richmond District

Golden Gate Park

One of the largest, finest parks-cum-cultural centers in world. No visit to the city is complete without taking in some of its wonders *(see pp20–23)*.

Union Street

A neighborhood shopping street loaded with tradition, Union Street is noted for its sidewalk cafés, bookstores, and designer boutiques, housed in converted Victorian charmers. The street is at the heart of the Cow Hollow neighborhood, whose name invokes its antecedent as a dairy pasture *(see p51).* ✪ *Map E2*

Pacific Heights

A grander, more exclusive residential area is hard to imagine. Commanding as it does heights up to 300 ft (100 m) overlooking the magnificent Bay, everything about it proclaims power and wealth. The blocks between Alta Plaza and Lafayette Park are the very heart of the area, but the grandeur extends from Gough to Divisadero and beyond. On a sunny day, there's nothing more exhilarating than scaling its hills and taking in the perfectly manicured streets, the

Typical house, Pacific Heights

Japantown

to-die-for views, and the palatial dwellings. The Spreckels Mansion, a limestone palace in the Beaux-Arts tradition, on Washington and Octavia streets, is the brightest gem of the lot, now owned by novelist Danielle Steele *(see p53).* ✪ *Map E2*

Japantown

The Japan Center was built as part of an ambitious 1960s plan to revitalize the Fillmore District. Blocks of aging Victorians were demolished and replaced by the Geary Express-way and this Japanese-style shopping complex, with a five-tiered, 75-ft (22-m) Peace Pagoda at its heart. Taiko drummers perform here during the Cherry Blossom Festival each April *(see p74)*. The extensive malls are lined with authentic Japanese shops and restaurants, plus an eight-screen cinema, and the Kabuki Springs and Spa. More shops and restaurants are found along the outdoor mall across Post Street. This neighborhood has been the focus of the Japanese community since the early 20th century. ✪ *Map F3*

Positively Haight Street, Haight-Ashbury

Haight-Ashbury

This anarchic quarter is one of the most scintillating and unconventional in the city, resting firmly on its laurels as ground zero for the worldwide Flower-Power explosion of the 1960s *(see p55)*. Admire the beautiful old Queen Anne-style houses, a few of them still painted in the psychedelic pigments of that hippie era. There are still some tripping freaks and Neo-Flower Children here, along with far-out shops and the venerable Haight Ashbury Free Clinic. Groove along the street and recreate your own "Summer of Love." The Lower Haight is noted for its edgy clubs and bars. ◈ *Map D4*

Flower Power

In 1967 San Francisco witnessed the Summer of Love, including a 75,000-strong Human Be-In at Golden Gate Park. People were drawn here – many with flowers in their hair – by the acid-driven melodies of Jefferson Airplane, Janis Joplin, Jimi Hendrix, and The Doors. Love was free, concerts were free, drugs were free, even food and healthcare were free. Soon, however, public alarm, and too many bad trips, caused the bubble to burst.

Hayes Valley

Rising like a phoenix from the ashes of racial unrest in what used to be a very rundown African-American slum, this small area has now become one of San Francisco's hipper shopping and dining districts. The dismantling of an ugly freeway overpass following the 1989 earthquake helped turn the tide, and the welcome result is a chic area that hasn't lost its edge. Hayes Valley festivals take place at midsummer, when the area's streets are thronged with revelers. ◈ *Map F4*

Geary Boulevard

One of the city's main traffic arteries, sweeping from Van Ness all the way out to Cliff House, Geary Boulevard is a typically unprepossessing urban thoroughfare, but functional. It begins its journey at Market Street, sweeps past Union Square, and then forms the heart of the Theater District, before venturing into the notorious Tenderloin, home to seedy clubs. After it crosses Van Ness, it zips past Japantown and the funky Fillmore District. Soon you're in the Richmond District and before you know it, there's the Pacific Ocean. ◈ *Map F3*

Presidio Heights

Originally part of the "Great Sand Waste" to the west, this neighborhood is now one of the most élite of all. The zone centers on Sacramento Street as its discreet shopping area. It's worth a stroll, primarily for the architecture. Of interest are the Swedenborgian Church at 2107 Lyon Street, the Roos House at 3500 Jackson Street, and Temple Emanu-El at 2 Lake Street. ◈ *Map D3*

9 Western Addition

This area, too, was once sandy waste, but after World War II the district became populated by Southern African-Americans who came west for work. For a short time, it was famous for jazz and blues clubs, as embodied, until his death in 2001, by John Lee Hooker and his Boom Boom Room. Today, it is still largely African-American in character and rather rundown, although it does comprise architecturally odd St Mary's Cathedral *(see p44)* and photogenic Alamo Square *(see p49)*. ◉ Map E3

10 The Richmond District

This flat district of row houses begins at Masonic Street, sandwiched between Golden Gate Park and California Street. It ultimately extends all the way to the Pacific Ocean, being more and more prone to stay fog-bound the farther west you go. The district is very ethnically diverse and generally middle class. Over the decades, it has been settled by White Russians, East European Jews, and latterly Chinese-Americans and another wave of Russians. ◉ Map C3

Russian shop, Richmond District

A Hippie Tour of Haight-Ashbury

Begin at **Alamo Square** *(see p49)*, with the Westerfield House at 1998 Fulton at Scott, former residence of Ken Kesey, the writer and visionary who arguably got the whole 1960s movement going. Walk up Scott, turn right on Page and go to No. 1090, where Big Brother and the Holding Company got their start. A block and a half farther on, go right on Lyon to No. 112, where Janis Joplin lived for most of 1967 *(see p55)*.

Continue on to the Panhandle, an extension of Golden Gate Park, where in June 1967 the Jimi Hendrix Experience gave a free concert. Now turn left on Central and head up to steep **Buena Vista Park** *(see p49)*, site of public Love-Ins in the 1960s and 1970s. Turn right on Haight and check out Positively Haight Street, 1400 Haight Street at Masonic, one of the fanciest hippie shops.

Continue on to the famous Haight-Ashbury intersection and walk along Haight to Clayton; at No. 558 is the much-loved Haight Ashbury Free Clinic, still imbued with the spirit of the 1960s. If you are tired or hungry, stop in for a snack at **Blue Front Café** *(see p105)*.

Refreshed, walk towards the park, turn right on Stanyan all the way to Fulton. At 2400 Fulton stands the former Jefferson Airplane Mansion, which used to be painted black. Finally, head back to **Golden Gate Park** *(see pp20–23)* and make your way to the drum circles on Hippie Hill to groove to the tribal beats.

Following pages: **Temple Gate in the Japanese Tea Garden, Golden Gate Park**

Left **Enchanted Crystal** Right **Polanco**

Top 10 Shops

1 Fatto a Mano
Unique home furnishings, including ceramics, glassware, and kitchen accessories. Owned by a husband-and-wife team, their beautiful handmade furnishings come from Italy. ◎ *1800 Union St* • *Map F2* • *(415) 525-4348*

2 Enchanted Crystal
This gallery/store offers an amazing collection of art, glass, handcrafted jewelry, and decorative gifts. ◎ *1895 Union St* • *Map F2* • *(415) 885-1335*

3 Carol Doda's Champagne & Lace Lingerie Boutique
Bodywear for women and men, brought to you by the infamous entertainment pioneer who brought topless dancing to San Francisco in the 1960s. Naturally, the emphasis is on risqué styles. ◎ *1850 Union St* • *Map F2* • *(415) 776-6900*

4 Brooks Shoes For Kids
This store specializes in high fashion with a huge range in all styles. Accessories and toys are also sold here. ◎ *3307 Sacramento St* • *Map E3* • *(415) 440-7599*

5 Past Perfect
Fair prices and tons to choose from at this huge vintage store. Plan to spend a while perusing their unique furniture, lighting, and art – there is something for everyone here. Friendly staff too. ◎ *2224 Union St* • *Map E2* • *(415) 929-7651*

6 Polanco
A sophisticated gallery of Mexican arts, featuring silver jewelry, colorful Day of the Dead masks and crafts, as well as the work of emerging Mexican artists. ◎ *393 Hayes St* • *Map F4* • *(415) 252-5753*

7 Marmalade
A chic yet casual boutique with dresses, tops, and jewelry that are stylish but not over-priced. Marmalade also sells fabulous bags, trinkets and other great gift items. ◎ *1843 Union St* • *Map F2* • *(415) 400-4027*

8 Comix Experience
Comics with adult aficionados in mind: *The Ring of the Nibelung*, *The Filth*, *Naughty Bits*, and *Static-X* are just a few of the whacky titles awaiting you in new and vintage issues. ◎ *305 Divisadero St* • *Map E4* • *(415) 863-9258*

9 Chronicle Books
More of a gift shop than a true bookstore, Chronicle Books is also a publisher and stocks its own titles. The store offers a large number of unconventional books as well as gorgeous cookbooks, and a wide selection of gifts. ◎ *1846 Union St* • *Map F4* • *(415) 345-8435*

10 Amoeba Music
Besides thousands of LPs, tapes, and CDs, there's also a huge selection of DVDs and posters. ◎ *1855 Haight St* • *Map D4* • *(415) 831-1200*

Price Categories

For a three-course	**$** under $20
meal for one with half	**$$** $20–$40
a bottle of wine (or	**$$$** $40–$55
equivalent meal), taxes	**$$$$** $55–$80
and extra charges.	**$$$$$** over $80

Above **Absinthe**

🏆10 Places to Eat

Perry's
A San Francisco institution, noted for its burgers and other all-American favorites, including meatloaf, prime rib, and fried chicken. 🌐 1944 Union St • Map F2 • (415) 922-9022 • Dis. access • $$

Hutong
The fantastic flavors of pan Asian and Pacific Rim cuisine, along with an exotic cocktail list, make this Wharf-area restaurant a popular choice. 🌐 2030 Union St • Map L5 • (415) 929-8855 • Dis. access • $$$

SPQR
Reservations accepted online only at this no-frills, rustic Roman-inspired eatery with mouthwatering antipasti and superior service. 🌐 1911 Fillmore St • Map E3 • (415) 771-7779 • Dis. access • $$$

The Grove
It almost feels like a mountain lodge, with lounging furniture and roaring fire. The tempting menu offers tasty entrées such as chicken pot pie or three-cheese macaroni. 🌐 2016 Fillmore St • Map E3 • (415) 474-1419 • Dis. access • $$

Pizzeria Delfina
Rustic, simple, and fresh, this popular pizzeria serves incredible Neapolitan thin-crust pizzas in addition to delicious, authentic antipasti and salami. 🌐 2406 California St • Map F5 • (415) 440-1189 • Dis. access • $$

Absinthe
This Parisian-style bistro serves specials such as confit of Muscovy duck leg with prunes. 🌐 398 Hayes St • Map F4 • (415) 551-1590 • Closed Mon • Dis. access • $$$

Suppenkuche
An ideal place for enthusiasts of hearty, meaty German food and beer. 🌐 525 Laguna St • Map F4 • (415) 252-9289 • Dis. access • $$

Kiss Seafood
Book ahead to eat delectable sushi and sashimi at this tiny restaurant. 🌐 1700 Laguna St • Map F3 • (415) 474-2866 • Dis. access • $$$

Blue Front Café
A local favorite for cheap, tasty Mediterranean wraps and sandwiches. 🌐 1430 Haight St • Map E4 • (415) 252-5917 • Dis. access • $

Nopa
Considered one of the best restaurants in the city, Nopa's menu changes seasonally. 🌐 560 Divisadero St • Map E4 • (415) 864-8643 • Closed L • $$

➡️ **Note:** Unless otherwise stated, all restaurants accept credit cards and serve vegetarian meals

Left **Castro District bar** Right **View from Twin Peaks**

Southern Neighborhoods

THE SOUTHERN PART OF THE CITY *comprises some of the liveliest, most authentic parts of town – the clubs of SoMa, the gay world of the Castro, and the Latino Mission District. There are also some up-and-coming neighborhoods such as Bernal Heights and Glen Park, as the more central areas have priced creative types out toward the southern borders. Laid-back Noe Valley was the first such choice for high-rent refugees, but it, too, has gone gentrified and pushed people farther south.*

🔟 Sights and Neighborhoods

1. San Francisco Museum of Modern Art
2. Mission Dolores
3. Castro District
4. Twin Peaks
5. Noe Valley
6. Mission District
7. South of Market
8. Yerba Buena Center
9. China Basin
10. Potrero Hill

Noe Valley church

Around Town – Southern Neighborhoods

106

Statue of St Joseph, Mission Dolores

San Francisco Museum of Modern Art

San Francisco's home for its extensive modern art collection is as impressive outside as it is adaptable and awe-inspiring inside. Don't miss the top floors, featuring the latest media, art, and digital installations, and the large-scale sculptures in the rooftop garden, including works bu Louise Bourgeois and Alexander Calder (see pp26–9).

Mission Dolores

The original Spanish Misión San Francisco de Asís, from which the city takes its name, is a marvel of preservation and atmospheric charm. It was founded in 1776, just a few weeks before the Declaration of Independence (see pp30–31).

Castro District

This hilly neighborhood around Castro Street is the center of San Francisco's high-profile gay community. The intersection of Castro and 18th Streets is the self-proclaimed "Gayest Four Corners of the World," and this openly homosexual nexus emerged in the 1970s as the place of pilgrimage for gays and lesbians from all over the country and the world. Unlike other cities, where homosexuals once hid themselves away in dark corners of anonymous bars, the establishments here have full-picture windows right on the street and are busy at all hours. Castro Street is closed off every Hallowe'en for the famous gay costume party and parade that most agree is one of the city's best, second only perhaps to the Gay Pride Parade (see p75).
◈ Map E5

Twin Peaks

These two hills were first known in Spanish as El Pecho de la Chola, or "The Bosom of the Indian Girl." At the top, there is an area of parkland with steep and grassy slopes from which you can enjoy incomparable views of the whole of San Francisco. Twin Peaks Boulevard circles both hills near their summits, and there is plenty of parking near the viewing point. If you're up to the climb, take the footpath to the top, above the main viewing area, to get a 360-degree panorama. The residential districts on the slopes lower down have curving streets that follow the contours of the hills, rather than the formal grid pattern that predominates in most of the city (see p60). ◈ Map E6

Castro Theater, Castro District

Noe Valley
5 Once a simple working-class neighborhood, the 1970s brought hippies, gays, artists, and other Bohemian types to its slopes and it soon became an attractive alternative to other, more established quarters. In its heyday it was known as both "Nowhere Valley" for its relative remoteness, and as "Granola Valley" for its nature-loving denizens. Lately, it has been taken over by middle-class professionals, who value the area for its orderliness, but 24th Street still hums with activity and is lined with cafés, bookstores, and the occasional oddball shop. ✷ Map E6

Mission District
6 The teeming Hispanic world, with all the accompanying noise and confusion, constitutes the Mission, home to San Francisco's many Latinos. They have brought their culture with them – bustling *taquerias*, salsa clubs, Santeria shops, lively murals, and Spanish everywhere you look and listen. It's a loud, odoriferous place, with edgy crowds dodging each other along the main drags, Mission and Valencia streets and their connecting streets from Market to Cesar Chavez (Army). Its *folklórico* festivals are not to be missed, especially the Carnaval *(see p74).* ✷ Map F5

A Gay City
After the free-love movement of the 1960s *(see p100),* homosexuals realized that they, too, had rights to stand up for, and started moving into the Castro in the 1970s. In no time the neighborhood was a non-stop – and unstoppable – party of freewheeling sexual excess. Suddenly gays were "out" in legions, which brought with it political clout. San Francisco is still one of the easiest places in the world to live out an openly gay identity.

South of Market
7 The city's erstwhile rough-and-tumble warehouse district has been on the rise for the last few decades and continues to attract arty types as well as a whole range of clubs and cool cafés. Plans are ongoing for more major transformations in the wake of the building of AT&T Park *(see p29).* ✷ Map R4

Yerba Buena Center
8 This area is fast becoming one of San Francisco's leading cultural centers for the performing arts, as well as a growing number of museums representing the city's ethnic diversity. Every year sees some new addition to the airy complex *(see pp28–9).*

China Basin
9 This old shipping port has not been exempt from the upsurge of interest in the previously neglected industrial area. The main change has been wrought by the building of the AT&T Park, home to the city's major league

Mural, Mission District

SoMa Esplanade

baseball team, the San Francisco Giants, and developers have already put forth ideas of how the zone can be put to use. A number of restaurants, bars, and clubs, many with port views, have opened up here or have been refurbished and gentrified. Ⓝ *Map H4*

Potrero Hill

At one time this usually sunny SoMa hill was set to become the next big thing. But somehow its isolation kept that from ever happening, cut off from the rest of the city, as it is, by freeways on three sides and its own precipitous inclines. Consequently, it has remained a quiet, pleasant neighborhood with spectacular views. To be sure, a few more upmarket concerns are located here, and there are restaurants and bars as well as many design stores, but mostly it is thoroughly residential. One tourist sight of note here is the Anchor Brewing Company. It's worth a visit, especially as the 45-minute walking tour and tasting session are free. There are only two tours each weekday; you must phone to book. Ⓝ *Map H5 • Anchor Brewing Co.: 1705 Mariposa St; Map H5 • (415) 863-8350 • www.anchorbrewing.com*

A Walk Around the Castro District

🕐 Begin at the city's gay mecca, the Church Street Muni Station on Upper Market. Decades ago, this corner developed a gay identity as the beginning point of the Castro neighborhood, but it is on the next block, between Sanchez and Noe, that the gay shops and venues really begin to proliferate.

Moby Dick *(see p68)* is a popular spot that attracts a crowd of regulars. Stop to shoot some pool or pinball while enjoying the retro tunes from the 1980s. Towards the corner of Castro is **The Cafe** at 2369 Market, offering a range of strong drinks accompanied by top 40 mixes to a trendy gay crowd.

Continuing on to Castro Street, take in Harvey Milk Plaza, with its huge rainbow flag, named after the slain gay leader *(see p39)*. On the opposite corner, check out **Twin Peaks** *(see p68)* at 401 Castro, the oldest totally "out" gay bar, notable for its picture windows affording a full view of goings on, both inside and on the street.

Pushing on to No. 429, allow the Castro Theater to capture your attention, one of the city's most ornate cinema palaces, home to innumerable premieres of gay-themed films. Farther along at No. 570, **Brand X Antiques** *(see p110)* is a great place to browse with its eclectic collection of goods, from furniture to homoerotica.

Finally, just up 18th Street at No. 4121 is **Badlands** *(see p69)*, a cruisy pickup scene that packs them in, especially after 10pm.

Left **Brand X Antiques** Right **City Art Gallery**

TOP 10 Shops

1 Needles and Pens
There's a little bit of everything here at this funky, ecelctic store. Don't miss the fantastic magazine selection, unique cards, stationery, t-shirts, and the gallery too. ⊗ 3253 16th St • Map F4 • (415) 255-1534

2 Jeremy's
A fabulous discount clothing boutique for men's and women's fashions, including Prada, Gucci, Armani, Ralph Lauren, DKNY, Dior, and Anthropologie – all at reduced prices. ⊗ 2 South Park • Map R6 • (415) 882-4929

3 Borderlands Books
A funky bookstore specializing in science fiction, horror, and fantasy. Whether these are your cup of tea or not, Borderlands is worth a visit for a dose of pure weirdness. ⊗ 866 Valencia St • Map F5 • (415) 824-8203

4 Brand X Antiques
The gay couple who own this shop have a discerning and humorous eye. In addition to baubles, rings, and furniture, the collection also features tongue-in-cheek vintage homoerotica. ⊗ 570 Castro St • Map E5 • (415) 626-8908

5 The Voyager Shop
A unique retail store of world-wide treasures, with everything from clothing and accessories to stationery and ocean gear, and a full gallery to boot. ⊗ 365 Valencia St • Map F5 • (415) 779-2712

6 Astrid's Rabat Shoes
If walking the steep city streets is challenging your footwear, this Noe Valley shop can fit you with a new pair of sturdy, stylish walking shoes. ⊗ 3909 24th St • Map F6 • (415) 282-7400

7 Paxton Gate
A wonderland of unique gift items and home décor, including strange bits of taxidermy. Kids love this place as much as adults. ⊗ 824 Valencia St • Map F5 • (415) 824-1872

8 City Art Gallery
This gallery sells work from dozens of local artists in a variety of media. Much of it is reasonably priced, making it a great spot to find a unique gift. ⊗ 828 Valencia St • Map F5 • (415) 970-9900

9 Botanica Yoruba
The Santeria religion is the faith of many Latinos, and this shop caters to their ritualistic and spiritual needs. An array of potions and powders, candles and icons (see p45). ⊗ 3423 19th St • Map F5 • (415) 826-4967

10 Candystore Collective
This adorable boutique features clothing and accessories for men and women, as well as home décor and gift items, most of which is designed and made locally. The store also functions as a small gallery. ⊗ 3153 16th St • Map F4 • (888) 601-0117

Left **111 Minna Gallery** Right **Make-Out Room**

⧉ Nightclubs

Café du Nord
Located in the landmark Swedish-American building, this subterranean nightclub is one of the city's smartest. It also hosts local and national bands. ✆ *2170 Market St • Map F4 • (415) 861-5016*

Make-Out Room
Cool live music and DJ nights make this a Mission favorite. The decor is original, the drinks are cheap (particularly during the nightly happy hour), and the staff is appropriately witty. ✆ *3225 22nd St at Mission • Map F5 • (415) 647-2888*

The Café
Something – and somebody – for everybody here at this camp, cruisy Castro old-timer that attracts gays, lesbians, and straights in equal doses. The outdoor balcony is great for people-watching. ✆ *2369 Market St at Castro • Map E5 • (415) 861-3846*

AsiaSF
Brazen Asian drag queens are your waitresses, who also perform bar-top and stage numbers. The tropical cocktails glow in the dark. DJs and dancing downstairs. ✆ *201 9th St at Howard • Map G4 • (415) 255-2742*

The Endup
Formerly exclusively gay, as famously featured in *Tales of the City (see p52)*, this classic is now thoroughly mixed, featuring house music, and an all-day Sunday "T" Dance. ✆ *401 6th St at Harrison • Map R4 • (415) 357-0827*

The Stud Bar
Around for over 35 years, this formerly exclusive enclave of maleness is now popular with anybody who likes a rollicking lusty time. Theme nights include Trannyshack, a fabulous drag cabaret show. ✆ *399 9th St at Harrison • Map G4 • (415) 863-6623*

111 Minna Gallery
Part gallery, part lounge, Minna is a fun place to grab a drink downtown, and there's almost always some event happening here. ✆ *111 Minna St between New Montgomery & 2nd • Map P5 • (415) 974-1719*

El Rio
Different dance events every night of the week draw a diverse crowd ready to work their thing – Sunday Salsa Showcase is popular. ✆ *3158 Mission St • Map F5 • (415) 282-3325*

Elbo Room
This two-story bar combines dancing, live entertainment, and pool tables. A great mix of people come together here for the welcoming atmosphere and a great time. ✆ *647 Valencia St • Map F5 • (415) 552-7788*

Mighty
Popular hip hop and house DJs keep the crowds dancing at this large nightclub, which doubles as an art gallery *(see p70)*. ✆ *119 Utah St at 15th • Map G4 • (415) 762-0151*

Left **21st Amendment** Right **Twenty Five Lusk**

Bars and Clubs

Lucky 13
A chill-out punk bar where you can sport your new tattoo to an admiring audience. The jukebox is full of indie alternative sounds. ✪ *2140 Market St at Church • Map F4 • (415) 487-1313*

Bottom of the Hill
This legendary live-music venue features an assortment of punk, rock and folk bands, plus a pleasant back patio for beer breaks *(see p70)*. ✪ *1233 17th St between Texas and Missourri • Map G4 • (415) 621-4455*

Nihon Whiskey Lounge
The white-pebbled floor and vast selection of hard-to-find whiskys make this Japanese whisky lounge a super-cool spot to grab a drink. ✪ *1779 Folsom at 14th • Map F4 • (415) 552-4400*

Twenty Five Lusk
Located in a renovated timber warehouse, this elegant bar-cum-restaurant is sleek and modern with a hip, urban vibe. The cocktails are delicious and the stylish lounge below is great for people-watching. ✪ *25 Lusk St • Map H3 • (415) 495-5875*

The Residence
Friendly bartenders keep people coming to this neighborhood hang-out with comfy chairs and a cozy, relaxed interior. There is a good selection of beer and cocktails. ✪ *718 14th St • Map F4 • (415) 797-8866*

Mezzanine
This richly diverse gathering space showcases live and electronic music from all genres – rock, dance, hip hop, soul, jazz, salsa, and world beat, as well as hosting multimedia art events and fashion shows *(see p70)*. ✪ *444 Jesse St • Map Q3 • (415) 625-8880*

The Knockout
With DJs and live music all week, and bingo on Thursdays, the Knockout has remained one of the most popular dive bars in San Francisco for years. ✪ *3223 Mission St • Map F6 • (415) 550-6994*

Trick Dog
Well-crafted and imaginative cocktails win rave reviews at this beautiful, split-level bar in the Mission district. Innovative decor and inspiring bar snacks. ✪ *3010 20th St • Map F5 • (415) 471-2999*

83 Proof
This popular neighborhood hangout is often crowded with locals, who come here for the inventive drinks made from the five shelves of liquors behind the bar. ✪ *83 First St • Map P6 • (415) 296-8383*

21st Amendment
A sports fan's dream, this brewpub near the ballpark serves up handcrafted beers and standard American fare. It's a friendly place to catch a game on television. ✪ *563 2nd St • Map R6 • (415) 369-0900*

Price Categories

For a three-course meal for one with half a bottle of wine (or equivalent meal), taxes and extra charges.

$	under $20
$$	$20–$40
$$$	$40–$55
$$$$	$55–$80
$$$$$	over $80

Above **Pancho Villa Taqueria**

🔟 Places to Eat

Delfina
Delfina serves perfect Italian fare. Its next-door pizzeria is ideal for a more casual dinner *(see p62)*. 🅢 *3261 18th St • Map F5 • (415) 552-4055 • Closed L • Dis. access • $$$*

Marlowe
This cozy yet chic restaurant serves outstanding bistro dishes. 🅢 *330 Townsend St • Map H3 • (415) 974-5599 • Dis. access • $$$*

COCO500
There is a relaxed and low-key vibe about COCO500 that brings visitors back time and time again. Try the fried greenbeans or the beef cheeks. 🅢 *500 Brannan St • Map H3 • (415) 543-2222 • $$$*

Sparky's Diner
Open 24 hours, this café is great for clubbers wanting to grab a late night breakfast or burger and fries. 🅢 *242 Church St at Market • Map F4 • (415) 626-8666 • $*

Chow
Just off Market Street, Chow offers affordable pizzas, pastas, grilled and roasted meats, beer, and wine. Friendly service. 🅢 *215 Church St • Map F4 • (415) 552-2469 • Dis. access • $*

Pancho Villa Taqueria
Pancho Villa is one of the best Mexican eateries, serving up authentic tacos and burritos for ridiculously low prices. 🅢 *3071 16th St • Map F4 • (415) 864-8840 • Dis. access • $*

Range
This sleek restaurant in the heart of the Mission District serves simple classics and is a perfect end to a day's sight-seeing. 🅢 *842 Valencia St • Map F5 • (415) 282-8283 • Dis. access • $$$*

Caffè Centro
A brisk business in drinks, pastries, soups, and salads. Always crowded *(see p64)*. 🅢 *102 South Park • Map R6 • (415) 882-1500 • Closed Sun • Dis. access • $*

Osha Thai
A perennial favorite with the club crowd. Dishes are fresh and tasty, service is lightning fast, and prices are extremely reasonable. 🅢 *819 Valencia St • Map F5 • (415) 826-7738 • Dis. access • $*

Stable Café
Stable Café serves delicious homemade breakfast and lunch options that center heavily on fresh-baked breads and healthy local ingredients. 🅢 *2128 Folsom at 17th • Map F5 • (415) 552-1199 • Closed D • $*

Note: *Unless otherwise stated, all restaurants accept credit cards and serve vegetarian meals*

Left **Legion of Honor** Right **Cliff House**

Oceanfront

AS WITH EVERY SEGMENT OF THIS CITY, *the area that faces the Pacific Ocean is a study in contrasts. Surprisingly to many, it contains terrains of natural beauty that are just as untamed and craggy as they always have been, particularly the rocky, windswept micro-climates that make up the cliffs and hidden ravines of Land's End. This has been the scene of innumerable shipwrecks throughout the city's history. Yet, just a few blocks away is Sea Cliff, one of the most exclusive residential neighborhoods in town. All up and down the area, beside blocks and blocks of tract homes, there are numerous parks and recreational possibilities, including, of course, surfing, if you're skilled and brave enough to face the unpredictable, freezing waters of the Pacific. Of all San Francisco's areas, this is the place where you're almost certain to encounter the city's infamous fog, but if the weather is clear there are great views of the offshore Seal Rocks and even the Farallon Islands. Further south, more activities can be enjoyed at Lake Merced.*

Koala, San Francisco Zoo

Sights

1. Cliff House
2. Ocean Beach
3. Legion of Honor
4. Oceanfront Parks
5. Seal Rocks
6. San Francisco Zoo
7. Sigmund Stern Grove
8. Sea Cliff
9. Sunset District
10. Lake Merced

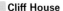

Around Town – Oceanfront

Cliff House
Built in 1909, the present structure is the third on this site and was renovated in 2004. Its predecessor, a massively elaborate eight-story Victorian-Gothic castle that burned down in 1907, was built by the flamboyant entrepreneur Adolph Sutro (his estate overlooking Cliff House is now Sutro Heights Park). Cliff House has restaurants on the upper levels, observation decks overlooking the Pacific Ocean, a wing containing two bars, and the Camera Obscura which gives a close-up view of Seal Rocks. ◈ *Map A3* • *Open for lunch and dinner (call for times)* • *(415) 386-3330* • *www.cliffhouse.com*

Ocean Beach
Most of San Francisco's western boundary is defined by this broad sweep of sand. Although sublime when viewed from Cliff House or Sutro Heights, the beach is dangerous for swimming due to its icy waters, rough shore breakers, and, most of all, rip currents that are powerful enough to drag even strong swimmers out to sea. Nevertheless, hardy surfers in thick wetsuits are a common sight, and in fine weather sun-bathers and picnickers materialize. ◈ *The Great Hwy* • *Map A4*

Legion of Honor
The creation of Alma Bretteville Spreckels, heiress to the Spreckels sugar fortune, this museum is a replica of the Palais de la Légion d'Honneur in Paris. The original temporary structure was built for the 1915 Pan-Pacific Exposition to house French art, but Mrs Spreckels wanted to build a permanent version and employed the same architect she commissioned to build her mansion in Pacific Heights *(see p99)*. It opened in 1924 and features a collection of medieval to 20th-century European art, with paintings by Monet and Rembrandt. The museum also hosts excellent traveling exhibitions. ◈ *Lincoln Park, 34th Ave & Clement St* • *www.thinker.org* • *Map B3* • *(415) 750-3600* • *Open 9:30am–5:15pm Tue–Sun* • *Adm*

Oceanfront Parks
Lincoln Park, Land's End, and Sutro Heights Park are large green areas that overlook and hug the coast all along this northwestern corner of the peninsula. Stupendous Lincoln Park is the work of the indefatigable John McClaren *(see p21)*, and features coastal trails affording some of the best views of the Golden Gate Bridge. Land's End is a surprisingly rugged and wild stretch along the coastal cliffs that features a stony, picturesque cove, stretches of broad sand, and truly spectacular hiking. Gardens, statuary, and walls of the old Sutro estate still decorate Sutro Heights Park, dominating the entire coastal scene from its dramatic vantage point. ◈ *Map A3*

Land's End

Discover more at www.dk.com

115

Seal Rocks

Seal Rocks

The westernmost promontory on this tip of the peninsula is Point Lobos, the projection that forms Land's End's rocky cove. Along to the south from here down to Cliff House is a scattering of small, rocky islands frequented by seals – hence the name. Bring binoculars to spy on the seals and birds in their natural habitat. At night, from the beach or Cliff House promenade, the barking of the sea lions – like the keening of the foghorns – is both reassuring and eerie, and so very "San Francisco." On a clear day, 32 miles (50 km) off the coast, you can see the Farallon Islands, also inhabited by sea lions and with a state-protected rookery. ® Map A3

Cliff House and the Sutro Baths

Adolph Sutro came to San Francisco from Prussia in 1851, aged 21 and looking for gold. Instead, he became the Silver King of the Comstock Lode (Nevada), and brought his riches back to the city to invest them in land. His projects included building the first Cliff House, the popular Sutro Baths, and his own lavish estate. In the process, he transformed the Ocean Beach area into a recreational gem. The legacy lives on, despite the disappearance of all three of the famous buildings he constructed.

San Francisco Zoo

San Francisco Zoo is at the far southwest corner of the city, between the Pacific Ocean and Lake Merced. The complex is home to more than 1,000 species of birds, mammals, and insects, among which 20 are considered to be endangered – most notably the snow leopard and Sumatran tiger. Gorilla Preserve, Grizzly Gulch, Koala Crossing, and Children's Zoo are particular hits, as are the feeding times for the grizzly bears and the penguins. Summer brings a busy program of extra activities in the Children's Zoo. ® Sloat Blvd at Pacific Ocean • www.sfzoo.org • Buses 18 & 23 • Open 10am–5pm daily • (415) 753-7080 • Dis. access • Adm

Sigmund Stern Grove

This 63-acre ravine in the southern Sunset District is the site of the nation's original free summer arts festival, endowed in 1938 and still in operation. The Sunday programs may include classical music performed by the San Francisco Symphony Orchestra, opera, jazz, popular music, or productions by the San Francisco Ballet. The natural amphitheater is in a eucalyptus and redwood grove. ® Sloat Blvd at 19th Ave, Sunset • (415) 252-6252

Sea Cliff

Many famous actors, such as Robin Williams and Sharon Stone have had homes in this élite residential enclave, which stands in stark contrast to the natural coastal area all around it. Most of the luxurious homes are Mediterranean in style and date from the 1920s. Just below the neighborhood, China Beach – named after poor Chinese fishermen who used to camp here – is one of the safest beaches in the city for swimming and is equipped with showers and other facilities. Baker Beach, just to the north, is another popular beach *(see p76)*. ◉ *Map C2*

Sunset District

Like its counterpart, the Richmond District *(see p101)*, this neighborhood was part of the Outer Lands and is purely residential, consisting of row upon row of neat, look-alike houses. Yet, like the entire area along the ocean, this district is subject to a great deal of gray weather. Its one claim to fame is Sutro Tower, the pronged red-and-white television antenna that resembles something out of a science fiction movie. ◉ *Between Sloat Blvd & Golden Gate Park and Stanyan St & the Pacific Ocean • Map C5*

Lake Merced

Located at the beginning of scenic Skyline Boulevard, this attractive lake, set amid verdant hills, extends across the southern end of the Sunset District. Relatively undeveloped and certainly under-used, it nevertheless gets its share of recreation enthusiasts. They come for the municipal Harding Park 18-hole Golf Course, and the biking and running trails that circle the lake's green shoreline. ◉ *Hwy 35*

Sunset District

A Two-Hour Hike Around Land's End

🕐 This section of the coast is amazingly wild, especially considering that it is actually within the city limits. Note that portions of the hike are very rugged, so dress accordingly, with good footwear.

Begin at the far end of the Merrie Way parking lot and take the steps down. Follow the trail that passes by the **Sutro Baths** ruins *(see p39)*, to your left as you descend. Continue on along to the Overlook, from which you can take in **Seal Rocks** and much of the Pacific panorama.

Now double back a bit to pick up the trail that continues along the coast. You will see the remains of concrete military bunkers, which have been broken and tilted by the unstable land, and now decorated with graffiti. Soon you come to a beach below rocky cliffs; note that the surging water is very unpredictable here, so be very attentive. Continue walking and you will arrive at Land's End Cove, where a makeshift beach, using rock walls as windbreakers, is popular with nudists.

Next, climb up one of the sets of wooden steps to join the path up above and continue on around the bend, where you will be greeted with a stunning view of the **Golden Gate Bridge** *(see pp8–9)*. Keep going all the way to Eagle's Point and return by way of the higher trail that winds through **Lincoln Park** *(see p73)*.

🍴 For a meal after your hike visit **Cliff House** *(see p121)*.

Following pages: **Baker Beach, with the Golden Gate Bridge in view**

Around Town – Oceanfront

Left **Williams-Sonoma** Right **Aqua Surf Shop**

🔟 Shops

1 Park Life
Part retail store, part art gallery, this sleek space features limited edition books, prints, homewares, jewelry, t-shirts, and art. The gallery exhibits contemporary art. ✪ 220 Clement St • Map D3 • (415) 386-7275

2 The Last Straw
This tiny store on the beach has been run by the same friendly owner for more than 30 years. Great, interesting pieces of jewelry, and unique finds. ✪ 4540 Irving St • Map A5 • (415) 566-4692

3 Gaslight & Shadows Antiques
The specialty here is porcelain, specifically the delicate masterpieces turned out by the various makers in the town of Limoges, France. It's like visiting a museum dedicated to this fine artform. Dolls and costume jewelry, too. ✪ 2335 Clement St • Map C3 • (415) 387-0633

4 See's Candies
Founded in 1921 by Charles See, this traditional shop offers high quality chocolates, truffles, brittles, toffees, and lollipops. ✪ 3250 20th St, Stonestown Galleria • Map G5 • (415) 731-1784

5 Aqua Surf Shop
Every sort of surf gear, including the extra-thick wetsuits needed to survive these northern waters. ✪ 2830 Sloat Blvd between 46th & 47th avenues • (415) 242-9283

6 Stonestown Galleria
Upmarket Nordstrom and all-purpose Macy's are the anchor stores to this traditional indoor-outdoor shopping center with the usual array of mall stores, from Gap to Sunglass Hut, and plenty of food outlets. ✪ 19th Ave & Winston Drive • (415) 759-2626

7 Green Apple Books
It is easy to lose a few hours browsing through the selection of used books and DVDs at this store. Part of the fun is taking the time to read the well-written and helpful staff recommendations. ✪ 506 Clement St • (415) 387-2272

8 Williams-Sonoma
The renowned kitchen, cookware, and serving-ware dealer originated in Northern California. Products from around the world, chosen for functionality and beauty. ✪ 3251 20th Ave, Stonestown Galleria • (415) 242-1473

9 Urban Bazaar
This cute shop features all sustainably made gifts and home decor items, much of it produced locally. The store often hosts local events including craft nights. ✪ 1371 9th Ave between Irving & Judah • (415) 664-4422

10 Paul's Hat Works
A one-of-a-kind store devoted to old-fashioned hat making. Each hat is custom made. ✪ 6128 Geary St • Map B3 • (415) 221-5332

Price Categories

For a three-course
meal for one with half
a bottle of wine (or
equivalent meal), taxes
and extra charges.

$	under $20
$$	$20–$40
$$$	$40–$55
$$$$	$55–$80
$$$$$	over $80

Above **Beach Chalet Brewery**

🔟 Places to Eat

Cliff House
Standard American fare, but
the real reason to come here is
to see the Pacific crashing on
the cliffs below and to witness
the wonderful sunsets *(see p115)*.
🚫 *1090 Point Lobos Ave • Map A3*
• (415) 386-3330 • Dis. access • $$

Beach Chalet Brewery
People come here for the
views – both of the ocean and
the murals – rather than the
food. 🚫 *1000 Great Hwy • Map A4*
• (415) 386-8439 • Dis. access • $$$

Outerlands
The menu changes to reflect
the seasons at this popular
beachside spot, but fresh baked
bread is always on offer. Grab an
outside table to watch the world
go by, or sit inside and marvel
at the reclaimed wood walls.
🚫 *4001 Judah St • Map A3 • (415)
661-6140 • Dis. access • $*

Ton Kiang
Many say this restaurant has
the best dim sum in the city.
Always fresh, hot, and tasty,
with various specialties. 🚫 *5821
Geary Blvd • Map C3 • (415) 752-4440
• Dis. access • $$*

Chapeau!
A memorably authentic
French bistro. The sommelier can
direct you to fine wines that pair
well with the classic fare,
including roasted pork loin.
🚫 *126 Clement St at 2nd Ave • Map C3
• (415) 750-9787 • Dis. access • $$$$$*

Kabuto Sushi
A great Japanese restaurant
– the sashimi melts in the mouth.
🚫 *5121 Geary Blvd at 15th Ave • Map C3
• (415) 752-5652 • Closed Mon & Sun
• Dis. access • $$*

Pizzetta 211
Thin and crisp pizza topped
with organic ingredients from
fragrant *aïoli* to home-made
sausage. 🚫 *211 23rd Ave • Map C3
• (415) 379-9880 • No credit cards
• Dis. access • $*

Q Restaurant
Friendly staff serve huge
portions of comfort food at this
local favorite. 🚫 *225 Clement St • Map
D3 • (415) 752-2298 • Dis. access • $$*

Java Beach Café
This cozy café serves sand-
wiches, soup, and pastries in a
nautical-themed interior. 🚫 *1396 La
Playa St • Map A5 • (415) 665-5282 • $*

Burma Superstar
A Burmese eatery with an
extensive menu. 🚫 *309 Clement St •
Map D3 • (415) 387-2147 • Dis. access • $$*

Left **Mormon Temple, Oakland** Right **Point Bonita lighthouse, Marin County Headlands**

The Bay Area

I N LOCAL PARLANCE, THE BAY AREA *breaks down into The City, the East Bay, Marin, the Peninsula, and the South Bay. Although technically Santa Clara and San Jose – and certainly Santa Cruz and Capitola – do not touch the waters of the Bay, psychologically they still embody the same liberal, open-minded ethos that so defines this area. This is probably because the dominant mentality of this swatch of Northern California is so definably different from those of Southern California and the Central Valley. In towns such as Berkeley, Mill Valley, and Stanford the emphasis is on progressive thinking; smaller enclaves such as Bolinas are determined to live life in harmony with the breathtaking nature all around them.*

Sather Tower, Berkeley campus

🔟 Sights

1. Berkeley
2. Oakland
3. Marin County Headlands
4. Sausalito
5. Mill Valley
6. Mount Tamalpais
7. Stinson Beach
8. Bolinas
9. Palo Alto & Stanford
10. Tiburon

Wellman Hall, University of California, Berkeley

Berkeley

Its days as "Berzerkly," when student protesters and tear-gas clouds filled the streets in the 1960s, are only a fading memory now, although Telegraph Avenue still keeps some of the counter-cultural traditions alive. A great university, "Cal's" faculty boasts some dozen Nobel Laureates, while beautiful parks, tree-lined streets, and unique shops typify this East Bay enclave. Berkeley continues to give more "power to the people" than any other US city, with a host of public services that puts other communities to shame. ◈ BART Berkeley

Oakland

Gertrude Stein's famous dictum about her home town, that "there is no there there," was challenged by a very proactive mayor, Jerry Brown, from 1997 to 2007 (see p39). Oakland's image, notorious for racial unrest and crime in the past, is being cleaned up to present a more visitor-friendly face, and there has been an influx of creative types who have moved here to flee the high rents of San Francisco. Oakland's attractions include huge Lake Merritt, which offers a range of recreational possibilities, a beautiful Mormon temple, and its Museum of California (see p126). ◈ BART 12th St

Marin County Headlands

To visit these raw, wild hills with aston-ishingly beautiful views is to enter another world; yet it's only half an hour's drive away, by way of the Golden Gate Bridge. The scale of the rolling terrain is immense, and the precipitous drops into the ocean dramatic. This is an unspoiled area of windswept ridges, sheltered valleys, and deserted beaches (see p76). ◈ Muni Bus 76

Sausalito

A former fishing community and now an upscale commuter area and tourist haven, this small town offers spectacular views of the city from its Bridgeway Avenue promenade. Historically, it has been an artists' town, with an eccentric mix of residents (see p54). Bungalows cling to the hillsides and boats fill the picturesque marinas, many of them houseboats that locals live in year-round. Excellent restaurants, accommodations, and some unique shopping possibilities, too. ◈ US 101

Marina, Sausalito

From Sausalito, the Call of the Sea is a tall-ship that sails on the Bay. Call (415) 331-3214 or look at www.callofthesea.org for details.

Great Bay Area Universities

Palo Alto's Stanford University is the Bay Area's most famous private institution of higher learning, inaugurated in 1891. However, in terms of intellectual clout, the University of California at Berkeley, the oldest campus in the California system, stands shoulder to shoulder, considering the number of Nobel Laureates on the faculty and its international importance. Stanford is known for business, law, and medicine, Berkeley for law, engineering, and nuclear physics. Both universities are among the most selective in the country.

Greek Theater, Mount Tamalpais

Mill Valley

Home to a well-known film festival, but perhaps more famous as the quintessential Marin hometown. It's wealthy, relaxed, and beautiful, and the well-educated populace is given to progressively liberal views on just about every topic. The old part of town is flanked by wonderful stands of redwoods, lined with old buildings that house restaurants and unusual shops, and the whole centers around an eternally pleasant public square where people come to hang out. ◈ Off Hwy 101

Mount Tamalpais

No more breathtaking view exists than that from the summit of mystic "Mount Tam," sacred to the Native Americans who once lived here. At 2,570 ft (785-m) high, those who hike up to the summit can take in practically the entire Bay Area at a glance. The area all around is a state park, a wilderness nature preserve with more than 200 miles (320 km) of trails that wind through redwood groves and alongside creeks. There are picnic areas, campsites, and meadows for kite flying. The steep, rough tracks here gave rise to the invention of the mountain bike. ◈ Hwy 1

Stinson Beach

Since the early days of the 20th century, this has been a popular vacation spot; the first visitors came on ferries from San Francisco and were met by horse-drawn carriages. Stinson remains the preferred swimming beach for the whole area (see p76), and nearby Seadrift is an upscale community of second or third homes of the wealthy. The stretch of soft sand here and the spectacular sunsets set off the quaint village, with its good restaurants and interesting shops. You can reach it via the coast route, but the drive up and over Highway 1 provides the most dramatic arrival, affording inspiring views as you exit the forest onto the bare headlands. ◈ Hwy 1

Bolinas

The next community up from Stinson is a hippie artists' village that time forgot. Intensely private, the citizens regularly take down all road signs indicating the way to their special place to keep visitors from finding them. Potters and other craftspeople sell their wares in

Discover more at www.dk.com

the funky gallery, organic produce and vegetarianism are the rule, and 1960s idealism still predominates. ◈ Hwy 1

Palo Alto and Stanford

An erstwhile sleepy university town, Palo Alto has experienced a boom as the focal point of Silicon Valley, and driving force of the "New Economy." Although a lot of the gilding has lately fallen off the lily, this town has been left with a considerably dressed-up appearance, as well as many fancy restaurants, hotels, and shops. The town is home to prestigious private Stanford University, with its beautiful, well-tended campus (see p78). ◈ Hwys 101 & 82

Tiburon

Tiburon is Marin County's less hectic alternative to Sausalito for its views and restaurants. Here, 100-year-old houseboats ("arks") have been pulled ashore, lined up, and refurbished, forming what is called "Ark Row," where you'll find shops, restaurants, and sunny cafés that enhance the charm of this waterfront village. There are also opportunities to observe wildlife in the parks along the shore, facing Angel Island and the city. ◈ Hwy 131

Tiburon

A Morning Walk Around Berkeley

🕐 Begin at the Berkeley University Visitor Center at 2030 Addison Avenue, where you can pick up information and maps. Follow around to University Drive and on to the university campus, passing Romanesque Wellman Hall, then take a left on Cross Campus Road. Straight ahead is the main campus landmark, the 307-ft (94-m) Sather Tower, also known simply as the Campanile, based on the famous belltower in Venice's Piazza San Marco.

Now continue on to rejoin University Drive and go around to the Hearst Greek Theater, venue for excellent concerts of all sorts. Next, head for handsome Sather Gate, which leads into Sproul Plaza, epicenter of the student Free Speech Movement protests that erupted into almost non-stop socio-political unrest in the 1960s and 1970s.

Exit the campus onto Telegraph Avenue, a kind of Haight-Ashbury East-Bay with radical vibes all its own. Cody's, at the corner of Haste Street, is Berkeley's most famous bookstore, and one block over is idealistic People's Park. Continue on back to Bancroft Way to pay a visit to the excellent University Art Museum and the Pacific Film Archive.

🖉 After your walk, head over to The Cheeseboard Pizza, (1512 Shattuck Ave at Vine St • (510) 549-3183 • Dis. access • $). The restaurant serves home-made vegetarian pizzas with creative toppings such as asparagus, gouda, and gremolata.

Left **Octopus, California Ecosystems** Center & Right **Gold Rush Artifacts**

TOP 10 Oakland Museum of CA Features

1 The Building
The museum building is an outstanding example of modern design. Opened in 1969, it is composed of reinforced concrete and consists of three levels of tiered terraces. To soften the angularity, roof gardens have been planted, accented with sculpture.

2 Natural Sciences
In the brilliant Natural Sciences Department, the state of California is presented as one of the world's top ten biological "hotspots". There are thousands of artifacts on display, including bird and mammal study skins and mounts as well as a huge collection of reptiles, amphibians, and fungi.

3 The Earliest Californians
Fascinating galleries explore early human history in the state, documented by materials such as basketry, stone tools, clothing, and rituals.

4 Mission-era Artifacts
An 19th-century icon of St Peter is just one remnant of the Spanish Mission years. You'll also find early colonial tools, and a section of a Spanish ship.

5 Gold Rush Artifacts
The lives of those who came to California from all over the world in the 19th century, hoping to strike it rich, are chronicled here. You'll see prospecting tools and rare mining equipment.

6 Earthquake Artifacts
A collection of objects that pertain to the 1906 earthquake are on display here, including porcelain cups and saucers fused by the heat of the fire that destroyed so much of the city.

7 California History
This section has exhibits associated with technology, agriculture, business, and domestic life from the early Natives to the 21st century. Events such as World War II, baby boomers, and Hollywood and Silicon Valley are also covered.

8 Art Gallery
The third level is devoted to the Gallery of California Art, featuring works by artists who have studied, lived, and worked here. Included are works by California Impressionists and members of the Bay Area Figurative movement. Check the website for details of the Art and History Galleries' opening times.

9 Photography
The Gallery of California Art also has a fine collection of the work of California photographers, including Ansel Adams, Edward Weston, and Dorothea Lange.

10 California Crafts
The largest collection of decorative work, including murals and furniture, by California Arts and Crafts practitioners Arthur and Lucia Kleinhaus Mathews.

Left **Roller Coaster, Santa Cruz** Right **Santa Cruz coastline**

Best of the Rest

San Rafael
1 Located in the heart of Marin County, this town has a charming historic center loaded with good restaurants and shops. When the street market takes over the main drag every Thursday evening, it's transformed into an impromptu pleasure fair. ✪ *Hwy 1 101*

Belvedere Island
2 This garden island, attached by a causeway to Tiburon, is one of the most exclusive residential areas in the Bay. It's worth a visit to take in the palatial homes and their sumptuous settings.

Point Reyes
3 This wild and windswept peninsula is a huge haven for wildlife, including a herd of tule elk, birds, and wildflowers. The area is also home to cattle and dairy ranches. You can watch migrating whales offshore from December to March. ✪ *Hwy 1 to Olema, then signposted to Point Reyes*

San Gregorio and Pescadero
4 San Gregorio, protected by cliffs, is the Bay Area's oldest nudist beach. Pescadero, in addition to having a state beach with wonderful tidepools, is also a lovely town that looks like something out of the Old West, complete with a whitewashed wooden church. The thriving farming community produces asparagus and pumpkins. ✪ *Hwy 1*

Woodside
5 This bucolic residential area is home to many of the Bay Area's first families, who built fabulous mansions here in the late 19th century. ✪ *Hwy 280*

La Honda
6 The most picturesque way to make the approach to the tiny community of La Honda and the Skyline Boulevard *(see p60)* is Old La Honda Road. ✪ *Hwy 280*

Los Gatos & Saratoga
7 These outpost towns still retain some frontier atmosphere, although they are now communities for the movers and shakers of Silicon Valley. ✪ *Hwy 280*

San Jose
8 This sprawling town is an integral part of Silicon Valley enterprises and has popular attractions. ✪ *Hwy 101*

Winchester Mystery House
9 The eccentric 19th-century home of the rifle heiress, Sarah Winchester, took 38 years to build and includes stairways leading to nowhere and windows set into floors. ✪ *525 S Winchester Blvd, San Jose • Open daily (call for tour times) • (408) 247-2101 • Adm*

Santa Cruz & Capitola
10 Some of the Bay's best swimming, as well as the famous Boardwalk, a vintage amusement park. ✪ *Hwy 1*

Left **Via Diva** Right **Stanford Shopping Center**

Bay Area Shops

1 Stanford Shopping Center

One of the first shopping centers in the Bay Area, this outdoor mall is dog friendly and features shops that you don't tend to find everywhere, such as Kate Spade, Free People, and Bloomingdales. ◈ *180 El Camino Real, Palo Alto • Hwy 101 • (650) 617-8200*

2 Powell's Sweet Shoppe

This old-fashioned candy store features row upon row of brightly colored gummy candies, chocolates, and lollipops, plus a number of vintage penny candies and novelty confectionery, such as bacon soda. ◈ *3206 College Ave, Berkeley • Hwy 80 • (510) 658-9866*

3 Gene Hiller

For over 50 years, this exclusive menswear store has been offering the finest imported designer clothing – including Zegna and Canali – from classic formal to casual. ◈ *729 Bridgeway Ave, Sausalito • Hwy 101 • (415) 332-3636*

4 Claudia Chapline Gallery and Sculpture Garden

In a great setting near the beach, the Chapline sculpture garden is full of delights, especially the brilliant kinetic pieces driven by the wind, which are the work of Lyman Whitaker. Inside, the variety and quality of painted and mixed-media work is very compelling. ◈ *3445 Shoreline Hwy, Stinson Beach • Hwy 1 • (415) 868-2308*

5 Via Diva

This collection of art and artifacts includes treasures from China, Indonesia, India, Thailand, and South America. ◈ *516 Irwin St, San Rafael • Off Hwy 101 • (415) 257-8881*

6 Treehouse Green Gifts

This eco-friendly store sells home accessories, garden items, and gifts for babies and kids, all by unique artists. ◈ *2935 College Ave, Berkeley • Hwy 80 • (510) 204-9292*

7 Tyler Florence Shop

The flagship store of local celebrity chef Tyler Florence stocks everything from homemade granola to specialty pepper mills. ◈ *59 Throckmorton Rd, Mill Valley • Off Hwy 101 • (415) 380 9200*

8 Convert

This trendy boutique sells men's and women's clothes and shoes, it focuses on sustainably sourced lines. ◈ *1809B 4th St, Berkeley • Hwy 101 • (510) 649-9759*

9 Shady Lane

The undertaking of a collective of artists who wanted to create a showcase for their work. ◈ *441 University Ave, Palo Alto • Hwy 101 • (650) 321-1099*

10 Global Exchange

Beautiful handmade creations from such places as Vietnam, Indonesia, Mexico and Senegal. The producers receive most of the profits. ◈ *2840 College Ave, Berkeley • Hwy 80 • (510) 548-0370*

Above **The Lark Creek Inn**

Price Categories

For a three-course meal for one with half a bottle of wine (or equivalent meal), taxes and extra charges.	
$	under $20
$$	$20–$40
$$$	$40–$55
$$$$	$55–$80
$$$$$	over $80

🔟 Places to Eat

The Lark Creek Inn
The redwood-shaded garden loveliness of this Marin hideaway is impossible to fault. The food is innovative New American cuisine such as roasted parsnip soup with black truffles *(see p63).*
🔊 *234 Magnolia Ave, Larkspur • Hwy 101 • (415) 924-7766 • Dis. Access • $$$*

Vasco
Vasco serves up delicious pizzas, pastas, and mouth-watering desserts. The downside is that there's nearly always a wait for a table. 🔊 *106 Throckmorton Ave, Mill Valley • Hwy 101 and Hwy 1 • (415) 381-3343 • Closed L • $$*

Las Camelias
Everything here is home-made and unusual. The decor is particularly appealing, most of the art being the work of the charming hostess-owner.
🔊 *912 Lincoln Ave, San Rafael • Hwy 101 • (415) 453-5850 • Dis. Access • $$*

The Bridgeway Café
Great for breakfast or lunch; you'll find a range of American favorites at this cozy little diner looking right out onto the Bay.
🔊 *633 Bridgeway, Sausalito • Hwy 101 • (415) 332-3426 • Dis. Access • $*

Parkside Snack Bar
Creative American brunch at picnic tables on the patio, or in the dining room. Try the Tomales Bay mussels in curry broth.
🔊 *43 Arenal Ave, Stinson Beach • Hwy 1 • (415) 868-1272 • Dis. Access • $$*

Chez Panisse
A very popular Berkeley spot which has been serving up excellent California cuisine since 1971. The upstairs café offers a cheaper alternative. 🔊 *1517 Shattuck Ave, Berkeley • Hwy 80 • (510) 548-5525 • Closed Sun • $$$$$*

Café Eritrea d'Afrique
An acclaimed restaurant serving Eritrean and Ethiopian cuisine in a relaxing and friendly atmosphere. They offer an all-you-can-eat veggie buffet on Wednesdays and Fridays.
🔊 *4069 Telegraph Ave, Oakland • Hwy 880 • (510) 547-4520 • $*

Alpine Inn
In a building that dates back to 1850, this greasy beer bar with a garden is popular with locals and Silicon Valley workers alike for its substantial burgers and fries.
🔊 *3915 Alpine Rd, Portola Valley • Hwy 280 • (650) 854-4004 • Dis. Access • $*

Buck's
After a long hike on one of the many trails in Woodside, enjoy a hearty Woodsider omelet and coffee at this kitsch restaurant.
🔊 *3062 Woodside Drive, Woodside • Hwy 280 • (650) 851-8010 • Dis. Access • $$*

Gayle's
This bakery and *rosticceria* has an extraordinary selection of gourmet treats – try the cappucino blend and to-die-for cup-cakes. 🔊 *504 Bay Ave, Capitola • Hwy 1 • (831) 462-1200 • Dis. Access • $*

Note: Unless otherwise stated, all restaurants accept credit cards and serve vegetarian meals

STREETSMART

SAN FRANCISCO'S TOP 10

Left **San Francisco Visitor Information Center** Right **Outdoor dining in the fall**

Planning Your Trip

1 Tourist Offices
Plenty of websites, representing the principal tourist agencies, tell you how to tackle the practical aspects of organizing a visit to San Francisco. You can also request that they mail you information *(see inset box)*.

2 Media
The city's daily and weekly newspapers – the weekly ones are free and super-abundant – are loaded with information about all the things going on in town. Perusing their websites will give you a head start on planning your trip.
⊗ *San Francisco Chronicle (daily): www.sfgate.com*
• *San Francisco Bay Guardian (weekly): www.sfbg.com*
• *SF Weekly: ww.sfweekly. com* • *Bay Area Reporter (gay): www.ebar.com*

3 Internet
Any search for places, people, or events to do with San Francisco will turn up a plethora of finds, but two sites give a good overview: www. sanfranciscocity search. com and www.baycity guide.com.The site www. redtricycle.com lists family-friendly activites and events.

4 Maps
San Francisco is very easy to find your way around, but study the general layout in advance. Free maps are available from tourist offices.

5 Visas
All travelers to the US need a valid passport, including returning US citizens. Most European citizens, as well as Japanese and a few others, need a non-refundable return ticket from outside the US to qualify for a 90-day visa. Travelers visiting under the Visa Waiver Program must register and pay a fee at https://esta. cbp.dhs.gov. Other nationalities must secure a visa, before traveling, from a US consulate or embassy.

6 Insurance
Buy a good travel insurance policy to cover lost baggage, canceled flights, and minor medical bills. The US generally does not have public healthcare so international health coverage is the wisest way to go.

7 US Embassies and Consulates
US diplomatic missions are found in virtually every country's capital. They can provide you with information about San Francisco, as well as answer questions about visa requirements.
⊗ *Australia: www.dfat. gov.au/missions • Canada: http://canada.usembassy. gov • France: http://france. usembassy.gov • Germany: www.usembassy.de*
• *Ireland: http://dublin. usembassy.gov/ • New Zealand: http://newzealand. usembassy.gov • UK: http:// london.usembassy.gov.uk*

8 When to Go
The nicest months are September and October. In summer, however, the coastal areas and the city tend to be blanketed in fog and points inland can be hot and dusty.

9 What to Take
Generally, San Franciscans dress casually. The best rule of thumb is to travel with as little as possible – if you're missing something, you can buy it.

10 How Long to Stay
Unless you are very unusual, you will fall in love with this city and want to stay as long as possible. A week should allow you to take in all the major sights; two weeks will leave enough time to explore the coast and the Wine Country.

Tourist Offices

Visit California
California Tourism, P.O. Box 1499, Sacramento, CA 95812-1499 • (877) 225-4367 • www. visitcalifornia.com

San Francisco Visitors Information Center
900 Market St • Map Q4 • (415) 391-2000

California Welcome Center
PIER 39, 2nd level • (415) 981-1280 • www.visitcwc.com

Streetsmart

Preceding pages: one of San Francisco's cable cars with Alcatraz in the background.

Left **Greyhound bus** Right **Amtrak train**

⑩ Getting to San Francisco

1 San Francisco International Airport

Fifteen miles (24 km) south of the city and linked by two freeways and a host of inexpensive public transport options, including BART, and private shuttles, as well as taxis and limos, SFO is very conveniently located and efficiently run. The airport has three terminals, and the largest international terminal in the US. Information booths are located downstairs and are open from 8am to 1:30am.
Ⓢ SFO: (650) 821-8211
• http://flysfo.com

2 Oakland International Airport

The East Bay's major airport is only a bit farther away from the city, so it can be a handy alternative. There are fewer crowds and a choice of transport to get you back and forth.
Ⓢ Oakland International Airport: (510) 577-4000
• www.oaklandairport.com

3 San Jose International Airport

If your destination is more Silicon Valley than San Francisco, you've come to the right airport. It's 50 miles (80 km) south of the city but only 20 miles (32 km) south of Palo Alto. Ⓢ San Jose International Airport: (408) 277-4759 • www.sjc.org

4 Customs

You're allowed to bring in 1 liter of liquor and 200 cigarettes duty-free, and $100 worth of gifts. If you're carrying more than $10,000 in anything negotiable, you must declare the excess.

5 Left Luggage

SF International has lockers in all boarding areas that you can secure for up to 24 hours. For anything bigger or that you want to store for a longer time, go to the Luggage Storage in the upper-level passageway between the South and International Terminals.

6 Lost Property

Each airport has a Lost Property service. If you leave something on public transport, there are numbers for each system, and taxi companies will also try to locate your possessions.
Ⓢ SF Property Control: 850 Bryant St; (415) 553-1377
• Muni (415) 701-5651
• BART (510) 464-7090

7 Greyhound

There are 10–12 buses every 24 hours from Los Angeles to San Francisco and back. It takes 8–12 hours but is the cheapest option. Greyhounds also go all over the US, but, although low in dollars, you pay in time and discomfort. Ⓢ Transbay Terminal • 200 Folsom St • 1 (800) 231-2222 • www.greyhound.com

8 Amtrak

The main Bay Area terminal for the US national railway system is in Oakland, offering a free shuttle bus to the city, stopping at the CalTrain station in the South of Market district and at the Ferry Building. The Coast Starlight route runs from Seattle down to Los Angeles daily, and vice versa. Ⓢ Amtrak: 1-800-872-7245
• www.amtrak.com

9 Shuttles

One of the best ways to get from and to the airport is to use the shuttle services, some of which are door-to-door. You can pick them up on the upper level at SFO. When making the return trip, however, you'll need to book the door-to-door type. Others leave regularly from major hotels and pick-up spots.
Ⓢ American Airporter Express: (415) 202-0733
• Bayporter Express: 1-877-467-1800 or (415) 467-1800; www.bayporter.com

10 Taxis and Limousines

Taxis can be taken from the lower level of SFO, and a typical journey into San Francisco will cost roughly $40, plus a standard 10 percent tip. Note that there is also a $2 surcharge for trips from the airport. Limousines are more costly and you will have to book them in advance.

Left **Cycling in Golden Gate Park** Right **Bay Area ferry**

Getting Around San Francisco

Cable Cars
Pure tourism, of course, but also one of the most enjoyable ways of getting around Downtown and Fisherman's Wharf. Pricey at $5 per ride, it becomes a bargain if you buy the CityPass ($69), which also gets you into many sights and is good for unlimited travel on the Muni transport system for a week from the time of first use. The Muni Passport can be used on the entire Muni system including cable cars.

Streetcars
The Muni Metro trams mostly run under Market Street and then make their way into the western neighborhoods. One line, the F, consists of vintage streetcars from around the world that decoratively traverse the Market Street circuit above ground.

Buses
To use Muni, you can either get the CityPass, or you can purchase Muni Passports for 1 day or 1 month, and for special events. The bus system is simple to use and will get you around this compact metropolis in good time, though rarely on schedule. Many bus stops have local bus route maps, as well as maps of the system as a whole. ⊗ (415) 673-6864 • www.sfmta.com/cms/home/sfmta.sfmta

BART
The Bay Area Rapid Transit system (BART) serves a large arc of San Francisco and connects it very efficiently with the East Bay. A convenient line also runs non-stop to San Francisco International Airport (see p133). BART stations are underground and many are shared with Muni Metro stops. ⊗ (415) 989-2278 • www.bart.gov

CalTrain
Since Peninsula residents voted against extending BART down south, this commuter train provides the most efficient public service to places such as Palo Alto and Stanford University (see p125). It is comfortable and punctual.
⊗ CalTrain Terminal: 4th St between Townsend & King • 1-800-660-4287
• www.caltrain.com

Ferries
The ferries provide wonderful, inexpensive excursions. The Blue & Gold Fleet serves Angel Island and Sausalito from Pier 41, and the East Bay and Tiburon from the Ferry Building. Alcatraz Cruises serves Alcatraz from Pier 33. Golden Gate Transit serves Sausalito and Larkspur from the Ferry Building. ⊗ Blue & Gold Fleet: (415) 773-1188; www.blueandgoldfleet.com
• www.alcatrazcruises.com
• Golden Gate Transit Ferry Service: (415) 923-2000; www.goldengate.org

Taxis
Due to a very tight licensing system, San Francisco does not have enough taxis, despite the poor car-to-parking-spot ratio. You can usually snag one by lining up at a major hotel.

Car
Rent a car only if you want to head outside the city. Driving here can be challenging to the uninitiated, and it isn't necessary for getting around, given the decent public transportation. Parking is also difficult. ⊗ American Automobile Association: 150 Van Ness Ave; (415) 553-7200

Motorbike
Motorcycling is a fast, efficient way to get around town. The same driving and parking rules apply to motorbikes as to cars. ⊗ Dubbelju Motorcycle Rentals: 689 A Bryant St • (415) 495-2774
• www.dubbelju.com

Bicycle
Scenic routes have been designated. It's a great, healthy way to take in the wonderful sights and parks, and convenient given the city's small size. ⊗ Bicycle Information Line: (415) 923-6164 • Blazing Saddles: Fisherman's Wharf; (415) 202-8888; www.blazingsaddles.com
• Plugz, electric bike rental: 550 North Point St; (877) 737-5849; www.plugz-rental.com

Organized tours of the city, Muir Woods, the Wine Country, and Monterey start at around $30. Telephone (415) 434-8687 for details.

Left **Parking instruction sign** Right **Waiting staff should be tipped**

Things to Avoid

1 Calling it "Frisco" or "San Fran"

Either say it all – "San Francisco" – or call it simply "The City." It's the name of a saint, after all, of whom San Franciscans are every bit as proud as they are of their city.

2 Driving Challenges

When you parallel park pointing up the hill, turn your wheels toward the center of the street; when pointing downhill, turn your wheels toward the sidewalk. That's the way to prevent runaway cars. If you are driving a manual shift rather than an automatic car, use your emergency brake when trying to start from a dead stop going up a steep hill – your mastery of the clutch under these extreme conditions may not be up to the job. The speed limit everywhere is 25mph (40kmph) or less, and all passengers must wear seat belts.

3 Underdressing

No matter how sunny it is when you go out in the morning, always take a jacket or a windbreaker. City weather is very variable and it will doubtless be cool, if not cold, damp or wet, by the time you return in the evening.

4 Unsafe Sex

For all its true sexual liberation, unsafe sex is always a no-no in this city that has seen all too clearly what can happen. AIDS and other STDs are a risk if practicing unsafe sex. Always use a condom.

5 Political Incorrectness

San Francisco is a city where diversity is embraced whole-heartedly, and supporting it is public policy. San Franciscans generally applaud differences of ethnicity, race, age, belief, gender, sexual orientation, and ability. Anyone who mocks or denigrates anyone else for any of these reasons has not understood what makes this city tick.

6 Smoking

California law makes smoking in any enclosed public place illegal – and that includes bars. Smelling cigarette smoke or even seeing someone smoking here is so rare as to be almost non-existent. If you must light up, there are back patios at some clubs where smoking is allowed, and some hotels offer smoking rooms.

7 Panhandlers, Petty Crime and Mugging

San Francisco does have more than its share of homeless people, and many of them do resort to begging. For the most part, they are merely annoying, not dangerous. However, pick-pocketing and purse- and camera-snatching do exist, and it's also true that certain areas should be avoided after dark. However, normal attentiveness should be sufficient.

8 Bad Neighborhoods

Even the seediest neighborhoods are pretty safe in broad daylight, but they, and parks, should be sidestepped at night, when muggings are most likely to happen. That said, there are very few areas that are really perilous within the city, but you should always be cautious.

9 Forgetting to Tip

Restaurant waiting staff depend on their tips to make a living – the salary paid is barely a tenth of what is needed to make ends meet. The usual gratuity is 15 percent, though you can reduce it to 10 percent if the service was not to your liking. Taxi drivers should be tipped about 15 percent, and hotel staff should receive $1 whenever they provide any sort of service.

10 Age Restrictions and ID

If you're over 21 but look younger, carry an ID with you showing your age if you want to try out some of the bars and clubs in town or want to drink alcohol in a restaurant or a shop. You must be over 18 to buy cigarettes.

Curbing your wheels when parking in the city is law-enforced – you will receive a fine if you fail to follow the practice.

Left **Discount museum tickets** Right **Discount ticket agency**

🔟 Budget Tips

1 Discount Air Tickets

In these days of deregulation and airlines squeezing out travel agencies, finding bargain flights is anybody's game. Most people find that the best bet is the Internet, but don't fail to contact local and national discount shops, too.

2 Hotel Deals

Again, trawl the Internet and sound out your local agencies to see what sort of promotions might be out there. Many hotels offer some fantastic bargains at certain times of the year.

3 Fly-Drive Packages

This sort of offer is somewhat superfluous if your main purpose is to get to know the city and little else outside it. However, if you want to dive into the fruit of the vine in the Wine Country *(see pp32–5)* or into the waves of the blue Pacific Ocean in Santa Cruz, Monterey, and Carmel *(see pp78–9)*, a car is a necessity. You may be able to negotiate a lower rate if you rent the car for only part of your stay.

4 Discount Coupons

The best discount coupon of them all is the CityPass *(see p134)*, which saves you a bundle, especially on public transportation, if your stay is for about a week. It currently incorporates nine additional attractions, including admission to the popular Exploratorium *(see p85)*, SFMOMA *(see pp26–9)*, the California Academy of Sciences *(see pp22–3)*, and much more besides. ◈ www.citypass.com

5 Cheaper Sleeps

Hostels, regardless of your age, are an excellent alternative in San Francisco. There are two locations run by Hosteling International, one in Downtown and the other between Fisherman's Wharf and the Marina. For budget beds also check www.airbnb.com *(see also p148)*. ◈ American Youth Hostels: (415) 863-1444 • www.norcalhostels.org

6 Cheaper Eateries

San Francisco has an amazing number of low-priced joints that often serve wonderful food. At some Mexican places in the Mission, you can have delicious *burritos* and *tacos* for under $5. Chinese restaurants and food trucks also offer many varieties of good value cuisine.

7 Picnics

With so many parks, having a picnic lunch is always a delightful option. There are plenty of deli-supermarkets, such as the Real Food Company and the California Harvest Ranch Market, which carry a fantastic selection of gourmet delectables. ◈ Real Food Company: 2140 Polk St & 3060 Fillmore St • California Harvest Ranch Market: 2285 Market St between Sanchez & Noe

8 Public Transport Passes

Muni offers 1-day, 1-month, and special event passes, all at great savings compared to paying $1.50 per ride on the buses and streetcars and $5 per ride on the cable cars *(see p134)*. The Clipper Pass is an all-in-one pre-pay travel card. It is accepted on most of the city's transport services including Muni, BART, and Caltrain.

9 Communications

Many services provide toll-free numbers when calling within the US from any phone – most of them begin with 800, 877, or 888. Buying phone cards to use for making toll calls can mean great savings. Internet access is free at the New Main Library and at CompUSA. ◈ New Main Library: 100 Larkin St; (415) 557-4400; www.sfpl.lib.ca.us

10 Laundromats

Nearly every block has a cheap laundromat handy. Wash cycles run about 15-20 minutes and dryers 20–30 minutes. Watch your things, however, since theft is not unknown.

For discounted hotel rates in the city, visit the websites www.hotels.com or www.priceline.com

Left **Disabled parking bay** Right **Muni streetcar**

ᵀᴼᴾ10 Special Needs Tips

1 Unlimited Free Parking
Nowhere provides more advanced facilities for the disabled than San Francisco. There are specially marked reserved spots for disabled parking, usually with a blue-and-white wheelchair sign and a blue curb. Often there's a blue-and-white wheelchair stenciled on the pavement, too. There's no charge for parking, either in these spaces or any other, as long as you display a disabled placard. ✆ *Department of Motor Vehicles • 1377 Fell Street • (800) 777-0133*

2 Special Prices
In addition to free parking for the disabled, all Bay Area transit companies offer discounted fares for disabled passengers, including BART, Muni, AC Transit, and Golden Gate Transit. National parks issue special passes for the disabled that entitle them and passengers in the same vehicle to enter free. In addition, many attractions offer reduced entrance fees to the disabled. ✆ *BART Passes Office • (510) 464-7133*

3 Required Accessibility
The San Francisco Visitor Information Center *(see p132)* publishes a free guide that indicates which hotels comply with the American Disabilities Act. However, if you

want to know the specifics, you should call in advance and ask a few pointed questions. In general, the newer the hotel, the more it is geared up to meet special needs.

4 "Kneeling" Buses
Only some of the Muni city buses have this feature, whereby the bus can be hydraulically lowered, allowing wheelchair-bound people to board, and then be secured in a special part of the bus. The "Muni Access Guide" will give you pointers on how to make the most of the system, and it is free from Muni Accessible Services.

5 Ramped Curbs
Wherever you go, all over town you will find that all the sidewalks have been provided with ramped access, at least at intersections, if not for every driveway as well. Ramped access is also standard for every major public building, including museums, concert halls, big hotels, government buildings, even ferries.

6 Accessible Toilets
Disabled-accessible toilets are provided in many places, including hotels and restaurants, attractions, and municipal areas. Some are inside the buildings, but there are also a number on the street – they are the green kiosks that you

can find at PIER 39, at Castro and Market Streets, and at the Civic Center, for example.

7 Independent Living Resource Center
This organization can provide every sort of information you might need about services for travelers with mobility problems, as well as for those with developmental disabilities. ✆ *649 Mission St • (415) 543-6222 • www.ilrcsf.org*

8 Braille Institute
This volunteer organization provides information about accommodations, museums, and other attractions that offer Braille placards and postings. ✆ *1-800-272-4553 • www.braille institute.org*

9 Seniors and Adults with Disabilities Line
Helpline providing advice and services for elderly people and adults with disabilities, including case management services and care-giver support. ✆ *(415) 355-6700*

10 Muni Accessible Services
If you have any questions about public transportation in the city, this is the number to call. This is also the place to obtain your disabled discount card. ✆ *(415) 923-6142 • www.sfmuni.com*

Left **Exchange office sign** Right **ATM machine**

Banking and Communications

Exchange
1 Exchange offices are found at San Francisco International Airport *(see p133)*, in some Downtown banks, and at American Express and Travelex America agencies. However, fees and bad rates of exchange are the norm. It's better to avoid the problem altogether by using ATM machines.

ATM Machines
2 For virtually all travel purposes, this is by far the best way to get cash, either through your home checking account or by securing a PIN number to use with your credit card. The rate of exchange is generally the best for that day, and the small fees charged by the banks are less than those charged by exchange offices. Best of all, you don't have to wait in long lines or carry ID.

Credit Cards
3 Paying with plastic is a way of life in the US. Use cash for small items, but pay for everything else with a credit card, if possible. Most hotels require a credit card number to book a room, and an imprint of one upon checking in. And you will not be able to rent a car without one. If your card is lost or stolen, call the toll-free number of your company and you will not be responsible for any further charges made.

Travelers' Checks
4 Nowadays these are more of a nuisance than a convenience. Cashing them in banks and exchange offices can be a time-consuming hassle. However, if you buy them in dollars, they're the same as cash and can be used for goods and services of any sort – but you may need photo ID.

US Currency
5 US banknotes are confusing as they are the same size and color. They come in denominations of $1, $5, $10, $20, $50, and $100, each with a different Founding Father or US president pictured. The coins are easier to tell apart, being different from each other. The 1-cent coin (or penny) is copper-colored; the 5-cent coin (nickel) is nickel-colored; the 10-cent coin (dime) and the larger 25-cent coin (quarter) are silver-colored.

Post Offices
6 Most US post offices are open from 9am to 5:30pm Monday to Friday and 9am to 2pm on Saturdays. Stamps can be purchased here, from some hotels, and from vending machines. If you need to mail something other than postcards and letters, wait in line at the nearest post office. Otherwise, drop your stamped mail off at the hotel desk or in any street mailbox.

Telephones
7 San Francisco's area code is 415, but neighboring localities have other codes. If you are calling from within the same area, you do not dial the area code; conversely, if you are calling from outside the area, you must dial the area code and precede it with a "1." From pay phones, calls cost 50 cents and up. Toll-free numbers start with 800, 877, 888, or several similar prefixes. For directory information, dial 411. International calls should be preceded by 011.

Voice Mail
8 The use of this service has reached epidemic proportions in the US, and you may rarely rouse an actual person. Leave a message, with a call-back number, then hope for the best.

Internet
9 There are many cafés that offer Internet services, usually from about $10 per hour. Many coffee shops offer free Wi-Fi.

Courier Services
10 FedEx, UPS, and DHL serve international needs, but you should also be aware that the US Post Office offers overnight delivery, both to major cities within the US and to selected cities abroad, and at much more reasonable costs.

There are $2 bills and $1 coins in circulation in the US but they rarely turn up.

Left **San Francisco ambulance** Right **Police car**

Security and Health

Earthquake Procedures

Should an earthquake strike, stay calm. If you are indoors, a good spot to stand is under a doorframe. If driving, stay in your car and park in an open place, not under a bridge or viaduct. If outside, try to get to an open area. Major quakes are extremely rare, but minor ones can happen and are mostly harmless.

Consulates

Most major countries have consulates in San Francisco. If anything untoward occurs to you, contact your national representative.

Petty Crime

This sort of thing does exist, so it's best to avert the danger before it arrives by being aware of your surroundings. Don't walk into less than salubrious areas, especially after dark, unless you're sure of where you're going or you're in a group.

911

Dial this number whenever an emergency of any sort comes up. It's a free call from any phone. Be sure to have all the information ready – where you are and what has happened – so they know which service to send out to you.

AIDS

This virus is still very much a public health problem. Throughout the Bay Area there are ample public health responses with a range of services, including free check-ups. Don't take risks – use a condom. ✪ *AIDS-HIV Nightline: (415) 434-2437 (English only) • California AIDS Foundation Hotline: (415) 487-3000*

Helplines

A number of helplines exist to provide support and information for almost any problem. ✪ *SF Rape Treatment Center: (415) 437-3000 • Suicide Prevention: (415) 781-0500 • Victims of Crime Resource Center: 1-800-842-8467 • Community United Against Violence: helpline for gays, trans-genders, lesbians and bi-sexuals (415) 333-4357*

Police Reports

If you are the victim of a crime of any sort, you should report it at your nearest police department. Especially if it involves the loss of money or any valuables, including credit cards, as you will need a copy of the police report in order to make a claim against your insurance.

Clinics

Walk-in urgent care clinics can be found all around town. ✪ *Concentra Medical Center: 26 California St; (415) 397-2881 • Haight-Ashbury Free Clinic: 1735 Mission St; (415) 226-1775*

Hospitals

San Francisco has several major hospitals, located in various districts. ✪ *Davies Medical Center: Castro St at Duboce; (415) 565-6060 • St Francis Memorial Hospital: 900 Hyde St; (415) 353-6300 • San Francisco General Hospital: 1001 Potrero Ave; (415) 206-8000*

Health Insurance Claims

Unless you go to one of the free clinics, you will have to pay for any type of health care you receive, and you will usually have to arrange for such payment before you actually receive the treatment. Also confirm that the hospital or clinic accepts your form of coverage.

Consulates

Australia
(415) 644-3620

Canada
(415) 834-3180

France
(415) 397-4330

Germany
(415) 775-1061

Ireland
(415) 392-4214

The Netherlands
(877) 388-2443

New Zealand
(415) 399-1255

United Kingdom
(415) 617-1300

Before you leave home make sure you understand how payments and/or reimbursements on your health insurance are handled.

Left **Picture market, Union Square** Right **Japan Center**

TOP 10 Shopping Tips

1 Department Stores

The big guns are all well represented in this city that loves looking good. Most of them are clustered around Union Square. The more upscale the department store, the more it feels like the exclusive parlor of some deluxe hotel, where you are the pampered guest. A very comfortable and luxurious way to shop *(see pp50–51)*.

2 Boutiques

The smaller shops generally feature more interesting and quirky merchandise – not counting all the international boutiques that also circle Union Square. Some of the more offbeat neighborhoods, such as Hayes Valley *(see p100)* and the Mission District, offer original designs, often by local or regional talents.

3 Malls

Only a few real American-style malls exist in San Francisco. They are the Metreon *(see p51)*, the Westfield Shopping Center *(see p51)*, and Stonestown Galleria *(see p120)*. Others are in historic structures such as Ghirardelli and The Cannery *(see pp12–13)*, or have architectural originality, such as the Embarcadero Center *(see p50)* and the Japan Center *(see p99)*.

4 Flea Markets and Thrift Shops

This sort of shopping can net you some real treasures and keep your bank account intact, too. One of the most central flea markets is in Bernal Heights. Thrift shops are all over town – two of the best are located in the Mission, the Goodwill Store and the Salvation Army Thrift Store. Both offer everything from vintage clothing to miscellaneous junk. ◈ *Alemany Flea Market: 100 Alemany Blvd at US 101, Bernal Heights • Goodwill Store: 1580 Mission St • Salvation Army Thrift Store:1500 Valencia St*

5 Garage and Sidewalk Sales

A thoroughly enjoyable custom that can unearth some surprising plunder in a city with so much style. To find a good garage sale, keep an eye out for announcements tacked to telephone poles, or take a weekend stroll in one of the likelier neighborhoods – such as the Haight, the Castro, and the Mission.

6 Bargaining

In established outlets bargaining is generally out of the question. However, in flea markets, garage sales, and some of the funkier ethnic stores, it is is acceptable. Make a counter offer and haggle it down to a mutually satisfactory sum.

7 Sales Tax

In the US sales tax is added to your total bill, rather than included in the listed price, apart from groceries. In San Francisco, the sales tax is currently 8.5 percent, and hotel tax is 14 percent. However, tax varies from state to state.

8 Corner Stores

Every two blocks or so all around the city, except in the most exclusive neighborhoods, there are corner stores that sell a little bit of everything – some fresh produce, maybe some deli items, a few toiletry necessities, and general groceries. Just be aware that you may pay as much as 50 percent more for everything you buy in a corner store.

9 Refunds

If you have second thoughts about something you bought, you have a right to return it for a refund. If it is defective, you are entitled to a replacement or a refund.

10 California Attorney General's Office Public Inquiry Unit

If you have been dealt with by a retailer or service-provider in an illegal way, you can take your complaint here so that court proceedings can be initiated or other sanctions put into effect. ◈ *1-800-952-5225*

For any unresolved complaints on a product you have purchased, call the Better Business Bureau on (866) 411-2221.

Left **Hotel grading sign** Center **Ice cream cake** Right **Clam chowder and sourdough bread**

TOP10 Eating and Accommodation Tips

1 California Cuisine

With over 5,000 places to dine and/or drink in the city, you know that food is important to San Franciscans. It's a moot point whether so-called "fusion" cuisine got its start in the city some decades ago but it has certainly reached its apotheosis here – with all the international influences, it was inevitable that chefs would begin borrowing and melding ingredients, flavors, and methods from a broad mélange of international styles. The result is California Cuisine.

2 Other Cuisines

It would be difficult to think of an authentic national cuisine that is not represented by at least one restaurant in the city. That includes Tibetan, Eritrean, Afghan, Kurdish, and Bolivian, as well as the more standard Thai, Vietnamese, Russian, and most European countries.

3 Reservations

If you're hankering after a fancy meal in one of the more famous restaurants, you'd do best to call in advance, sometimes up to two months ahead in the case of one or two of the top Bay Area draws. For the middling places, making a reservation a day or two before should suffice, unless you choose a weekend night.

4 Drinks

Good restaurants have *sommeliers*, so you can usually depend on their wine choices to go with what you have ordered. If you choose your own wine, remember that California wines are identified by grape rather than by region. If beer is more your thing, there are excellent local brews that compete very well with the best European products. And don't forget to try the local mineral waters *(see p67)*.

5 Tax and Tipping

Sales tax applies to restaurants, so 8.5 percent will be added to your total check. You should leave at least a 15 percent tip *(see p135)*. You may add the tip to your credit card slip, or leave it in cash on the table.

6 Choosing Hotel Locations

Do you want to be right in the heart of the action? Do you want a view of the Bay? Do you want to experience one of the unique neighborhoods? Once you've decided, you can zero in on the right price-range *(see pp142–9)*.

7 Hotel Gradings

Accommodations of every sort are to be found in the city and its environs. There is a star-based grading system, which pertains to certain amenities, such as telephone, TV, mini bar, etc.

8 Making Hotel Reservations

San Francisco is a popular destination and hotels generally fill up quickly in almost every price category. Don't waste a moment securing a reservation. Telephone bookings are accepted with a valid credit card.

9 Extra Costs and Tipping

Parking at Downtown hotels is almost always extra, paid on a per night basis, and a flat fee of up to $1 (sometimes more) is charged for each phone call made from the room, even if it is a toll-free number. Anything you take from a mini bar will be surcharged. You will receive an itemized bill when you check out. Tipping is important for any service provided *(see p135)*.

10 Traveling with Kids

Many hotels levy no extra charge for children under 12 staying in their parents' room, and some raise the age as high as 18 – ask in advance. However, some charge an extra $10–$45 for a roll-away bed and charge for a child of any age. Some of the best family-friendly accommodations are found among the motels along the Marina and in the Fisherman's Wharf area, where parking is usually included too.

Left **Fairmont Hotel** Right **Mark Hopkins Inter-Continental**

🔟 Hilltop Hotels

1 The Ritz-Carlton
If you want the ultimate in luxury and thoughtful service, this is the place to come. The views from the perfectly appointed rooms are magnificent, the staff at the top of their game, and the food sublime. 🌊 600 Stockton St • Map N4 • (415) 296-7465 • www.ritzcarlton.com • Dis. access • $$$$$

2 Mark Hopkins Inter-Continental
The Top of the Mark restaurant is a major pull, of course, with its 360-degree panorama, and the service is genuinely caring. The rooms are provided with every amenity and achieve an excellent standard of comfort. 🌊 1 Nob Hill • Map N3 • (415) 392-3434 • www.markhopkins.net • Dis. access • $$$$

3 Fairmont
"Opulent" and "palatial" barely begin to describe this grande dame of San Francisco hotels, taking pride of place on Nob Hill. The rooms and service are commensurate with its status. 🌊 950 Mason St • Map N3 • (415) 772-5000 • www.fairmont.com • Dis. access • $$$$

4 Stanford Court Renaissance
Long a business favorite, it's just near the top of Nob Hill and handy to everything Downtown.

The stained-glass dome in the lobby gives it a grand feel. Marble baths and canopy beds in some rooms, and every comfort seen to. 🌊 905 California St • Map N3 • (415) 989-3500 • www.renaissancehotels.com • $$$$

5 Huntington
Situated at the top of Nob Hill, across from Grace Cathedral, this hotel is like staying in the clubby apartment of a rich uncle with impeccable taste. The rooms are luxurious, there's an excellent restaurant, and a spa where you can get a champagne facial. 🌊 1075 California St • Map N3 • (415) 474-5400 • www.huntingtonhotel.com • $$$$

6 Laurel Inn
This stylish hotel is located in Presidio Heights, and is decorated in a hip mid-century fashion. The rooms have kitchenettes and some feature CD and DVD players. Breakfast is included and there is free parking. 🌊 444 Presidio Ave • Map E3 • (415) 567-8467 • www.jdvhospitality.com • Dis. access • $$$

7 Hotel Drisco
This Pacific Heights property is one of the Leading Small Hotels of the World, and, although the elegance is perhaps a little too understated, it delivers on service.

Details include complimentary breakfast and morning newspaper – and some of the very best vistas in the city. 🌊 2901 Pacific Ave • Map E2 • (415) 346-2880 • www.hoteldrisco.com • Dis. access • $$$

8 Queen Anne
Built in 1890, this old mansion has been lovingly refurbished according to Victorian taste. Rooms are all different and filled with antiques. Breakfast is complimentary, and your morning newspaper, too. The views are delightful. 🌊 1590 Sutter at Octavia • Map F3 • (415) 441-2828 • www.queenanne.com • Dis. access • $$

9 Hotel Sausalito
This warm, inviting boutique hotel offers luxurious rooms and suites with park and harbor views. 🌊 16 El Portal (at Bridgeway), Sausalito • (415) 332-0700 • Dis. access • $$

10 Claremont Resort and Spa
This country club-style resort in the Berkeley Hills was built in 1915 and still retains the feel of that era. There are business services, a fitness center, two pools, tennis courts, and views of Golden Gate Bridge. 🌊 41 Tunnel Rd, Berkeley • (510) 843-3000 • www.claremontresort.com • Dis. access • $$$

Note: Unless otherwise stated, all hotels accept credit cards, and have en-suite bathrooms and air conditioning

Price Categories

For a standard, double room per night (with breakfast if included), taxes and extra charges.

$	under $100
$$	$100–$200
$$$	$200–$250
$$$$	$250–$300
$$$$$	over $300

Above **Lobby, Hyatt Regency**

🔟 Traditional Hotels

1 Mandarin Oriental
Located on the top 11 floors of Downtown's third-tallest building, this is one of the classiest hotels in the city. Its East-meets-West decor is elegant, its restaurant one of the finest, and the rooms, amenities, and service superb. Splendid views. ◎ *222 Sansome St • Map N5 • (415) 276-9888 • www.mandarinoriental. com • Dis. access • $$$$$*

2 JW Marriott Hotel
It's all about location at this large, elegant Union Square hotel. Rooms have all amenities and people rave about the pillow-top beds. Service is top-notch and lounge areas in the lobby are welcoming, relaxing, and beautifully furnished. ◎ *500 Post St • Map P3 • (415) 771-8600 • www.jw marriottunionsquare.com • Dis. access • $$$*

3 Palace
Dating from 1875, this historic landmark emanates an aura of architectural splendor that nevertheless whispers refinement. The stupefyingly gorgeous Garden Court and the original Maxfield Parrish mural in the Pied Piper Lounge are national treasures. The rooms are wonderful, too, but many sadly without views. ◎ *2 New Montgomery St • Map P5 • (415) 512-1111 • www.sfpalace.com • Dis. access • $$$*

4 Le Meridien
Sleek and sophisticated, Le Meridien is an elegant hotel with many rooms having views of the bay. Its restaurant, The Park Grill, serves American cuisine and has a lovely outdoor patio for dining. The terrace is also a great place to enjoy drinks. Service is first-class. ◎ *333 Battery St • Map N5 • (415) 296-2900 • www.starwoodhotels. com • Dis. access • $$$$*

5 Sir Francis Drake
Where the doormen wear Beefeater costumes and the cable cars glide by constantly. This splendid Art Deco landmark is just a block off Union Square. All in all, a very festive and colorful feel, both in the public and private rooms. ◎ *450 Powell St • Map P4 • (415) 392-7755 • www.sirfrancis drake.com • Dis. access • $$$*

6 Hotel Nikko
High-tech and minimalist white marble interiors radiate modernity in this Japanese-style environment. Its cool comfort and tranquil luxury, such as silk wallpaper, soothe the spirit and free the mind. The excellent Anzu restaurant creates the same peaceful atmosphere. ◎ *222 Mason St • Map Q3 • (415) 394-1111 • www.hotelnikkosf.com • Dis. access • $$$*

7 Hyatt Regency
The 15-story lobby has long plants trailing down, a waterfall, and glass elevators. Try the revolving restaurant on the roof for its views. ◎ *50 Drumm St • Map N6 • (415) 788-1234 • www. sanfranciscoregencyhyatt. com • Dis. access • $$$$*

8 Four Seasons
Designed with the expense-account traveler in mind, this place has every sort of business amenity, including two phone lines with a high-speed Internet connection in each room, and a well-run business center. ◎ *757 Market St • Map P4 • (415) 633-3000 • www.fourseasons.com • Dis. access • $$$$$*

9 The Westin St Francis
This grand San Francisco institution still shines in its public rooms, but it's become a tour-group mediocrity otherwise. The tower rooms have phenomenal views. ◎ *335 Powell St • Map P4 • (415) 397-7000 • www.westin. com • Dis. access • $$$*

10 Ritz-Carlton Resort
A rambling mansion on its own verdant bluff, overlooking the Pacific. The perfect retreat from which to enjoy the Bay Area. ◎ *1 Miramontes Point Rd, Half Moon Bay • (650) 712-7000 • www.ritzcarlton.com • Dis. access • $$$$$*

Left **Taj Campton Place** Right **The Clift**

🔟 Boutique Hotels

1 Taj Campton Place
A member of the Leading Small Hotels of the World and definitely one of San Francisco's finest, this place aims to provide personal attention to every guest. Expect to find the best of everything. Its restaurant, serving California cuisine, also has national ranking. 🕲 *340 Stockton St • Map P4 • (415) 781-5555 • www.camptonplace.com • Dis. access • $$$$$*

2 Hotel Monaco
In the heart of the Theater District, this quirky but extremely comfortable hotel is run to perfection. The fairy-tale decor is joyously original, being at once a celebration of color and elegance, and the beds may be the most comfortable in the world. The stylish restaurant is an attraction in itself. 🕲 *501 Geary St • Map P3 • (415) 292-0100 • www.monaco-sf.com • Dis. access • $$$*

3 W
Talk about trendy in this town, and all conversations will lead to the W hotel. Minimalist with luxury touches throughout. Rooms have cordless phones and CD players. The clientele that come for drinks are chic trendsetters too. 🕲 *181 3rd St • Map Q5 • (415) 777-5300 • www.starwoodhotels. com • Dis. access • $$$$*

4 The Clift
"Equal parts wit, surrealism, and glamour." So say the proprietors of this Ian Schrager property, with interiors by Philippe Starck. You'll laugh with delight at the visual jokes, including a *chaise* very, very *longue* by none other than Dalí. 🕲 *495 Geary St • Map P3 • (415) 775-4700 • www. morganshotelgroup.com • Dis. access • $$$*

5 Hotel Triton
Perhaps the city's most original hotel, featuring avant-garde touches – evening tarot card readings, feather boa rentals, and several suites designed by rock celebrities, including Jerry Garcia. It's all too cool for words; you might run into Cher or Courtney Love, both of whom have stayed here. 🕲 *342 Grant Ave • Map P4 • (415) 394-0500 • www.hoteltriton.com • Dis. access • $$*

6 Hotel Rex
Steeped in California's literary and artistic traditions, this great little hotel boasts an intellectual air and decor that suggest 1920s salon society. Still, the rooms have the very latest touches, as well as writing desks for guests to pursue their own creativity. 🕲 *562 Sutter St • Map P3 • (415) 433-4434 • www.thehotelrex.com • Dis. access • $$$*

7 Inn at the Presidio
Housed in an historic building in the heart of Presidio close to fabulous restaurants and museums, this elegant hotel has beautifully appointed yet simple rooms. 🕲 *42 Moraga Ave • Map D2 • (415) 800-7356 • www. innatthepresidio.com • Dis. access • $$$*

8 The Inn Above Tide
The only hotel built directly onto the Bay. The views from guestroom balconies are stunning, and the ambiance serene. A wonderful choice, convenient to the city via the Golden Gate Bridge or a ferry ride. 🕲 *30 El Portal, Sausalito • (415) 332-9535 • www. innabovetide.com • Dis. access • $$$$*

9 Mill Valley Inn
Combining the sophistication of a European hotel – tea is served all day – with the cozy charm of a California mill town, tucked away in a redwood grove. 🕲 *165 Throckmorton Ave, Mill Valley • (415) 389-6608 • www.marinhotels.com • $$*

10 Garden Court Hotel
Elegant, remodeled guestrooms feature private terraces in this Spanish-style hotel. 🕲 *520 Cowper St, Palo Alto • (650) 322-9000 • www.gardencourt.com • Dis. access • $$$*

Note: *Unless otherwise stated, all hotels accept credit cards, and have en suite bathrooms and air conditioning*

Above **The Red Victorian**

Price Categories

For a standard, double room per night (with breakfast if included), taxes and extra charges.	**$** under $100
	$$ $100–$200
	$$$ $200–$250
	$$$$ $250–$300
	$$$$$ over $300

🔟 B&Bs and Guesthouses

1 White Swan Inn
This quaint B&B is like a country inn in the heart of Downtown, with bright floral prints, Victorian-style canopied beds, and warm, cozy fireplaces. An evening wine reception and a great English breakfast are complimentary. ⚅ 845 Bush St • Map N3 • (415) 775-1755 • www.whiteswaninnsf.com • $$

2 The Union Street Inn
Combining the elegance and gentility of an Edwardian home, just up from the Marina and right on fashionable Union Street. The individually decorated rooms are all spacious, with original antiques and art, fine linens, and complimentary chocolates, fresh flowers, and fruit. ⚅ 2229 Union St • Map E2 • (415) 346-0424 • www.unionstreetinn.com • $$$

3 Hotel Vitale
The amenities reign supreme at this urban oasis looming above the city's spectacular waterfront. Check out your preferred style of pillow in the pillow library, attend a complimentary morning yoga class, relax in one of the outdoor rooftop soaking tubs, or enjoy luxury spa services. ⚅ 8 Mission St • Map H2 • (415) 278-3700 • www.hotelvitale.com • Dis. access • $$$$$

4 The Red Victorian
Inspired along hippie ideals, you meet the owners and other guests and engage in intelligent conversation at the breakfast table at the "Peace Café". Each guestroom is also designed to celebrate an aspect of world love. ⚅ 1665 Haight St • Map E4 • (415) 864-1978 • www.redvic.com • No air conditioning • $

5 Cavallo Point Lodge
A former military base, this luxury lodge has the charm of a B&B and is set in beautiful surroundings at the foot of the Golden Gate Bridge. Rooms are comfortable and spacious. ⚅ 601 Murray Circle, Fort Baker, Sausalito • (415) 339-4700 • www.cavallopoint.com • Dis. access • No air conditioning • $$$$

6 Mountain Home Inn
Step out of the door of this quaint mountainside inn and be blown away by the spectacular views of San Francisco Bay and Mt Tamalpais. Just 20 minutes from downtown, this hiker's paradise invites you to meander to the beachside town of Stinson or to historic Muir Woods. Afterwards, indulge in hearty gourmet meals. ⚅ 810 Panoramic Hwy, Mill Valley • (415) 381-9000 • www.mtnhomeinn.com • Dis. access • $$$$

7 Sleep Over Sauce
This guest house is a great find in the bustle of the city. Rooms are clean, modern, and comfortable. Its restaurant, Sauce, is award winning. ⚅ 135 Gough St • Map F4 • (415) 621-0896 • www.sleepsf.com • Dis. access • No air conditioning • $$

8 Panama Hotel
A friendly, eccentric place, filled with period eclectic touches. Rooms have names such as the Bordello Room, and the Captain's Cabin – each with its own tale to tell. Pets are welcome. ⚅ 4 Bayview St, San Rafael • (415) 457-3993 • www.panamahotel.com • No air conditioning • $$

9 The Pelican Inn
Majestically positioned deep in a valley, each of the seven rooms has antiques, and a roaring fire is lit every day in the inglenook fireplace. ⚅ 10 Pacific Way, Muir Beach • (415) 383-6000 • www.pelicaninn.com • No air conditioning • $$$

10 Cliff Crest B&B Inn
Surrounded by redwoods, the rooms in this Queen Anne Victorian are graced with fresh flowers, and some have views of the Bay. ⚅ 407 Cliff St, Santa Cruz • (831) 252-1057 • www.cliffcrestinn.com • No air conditioning • Dis. access • $$

Left **Hotel del Sol** Right **Tuscan Inn**

Top 10 Neighborhood Hotels

1 Hotel Del Sol
Called "festive and spacious," this boutique hotel really is a ray of sunshine. Bright colors and cheerful patterns greet you around every corner, and the staff is just as nice as can be. An especially great place to bring the kids. ✆ 3100 Webster St • Map E2 • (415) 921-5520 • www.thehoteldelsol.com • No air conditioning • $$

2 Hotel Mirabelle
Located in the hip, urban Mission District, this charming renovated Victorian guesthouse offers a genuine neighborly customer service. It has a relaxed and welcoming atmosphere with complimentary breakfast. Shared bathrooms explain the bargain price. ✆ 1906 Mission St • Map F4 • (415) 377-4170 • No en-suite bathrooms • No air conditioning • www.hotelmirabelle.com • $

3 Marina Motel
Tucked away in a flower-filled Mediterranean courtyard decorated with murals, this motel offers guests a peaceful oasis right in the heart of the beautiful Marina District, close to restaurants and public transport. Rooms are simple and clean, and parking is included. ✆ 2576 Lombard St • Map E2 • (415) 921-9406 or 1-800 346-6118 • www.marinamotel.com • $$

4 Stanyan Park Hotel
Listed on the National Register of Historic Places, this Victorian hotel has been receiving guests since 1904. It is located right on Golden Gate Park and is decorated in period style. Continental breakfast is included. ✆ 750 Stanyan St • Map D4 • (415) 751-1000 • www.stanyanpark.com • No air conditioning • Dis. access • $$

5 Phoenix Hotel
Johnny Depp, REM, and the late John F. Kennedy, Jr have all stayed here. Located a bit too close to the Tenderloin for all but the most self-assured. Continental breakfast is included, and the popular restaurant/bar draws hipsters from all over the city. ✆ 601 Eddy St • Map Q2 • (415) 776-1380 • www.jdvhospitality.com • Dis. access • $$

6 Tuscan Inn
It's part of the Best Western chain, but don't let that put you off as it's one of the stylish ones. Located right in Fisherman's Wharf, staying here takes some of the touristy edge off the neighborhood. Features include a mirrored wall in each room, and free coffee and tea. ✆ 425 North Point St • Map K3 • (415) 561-1100 • www.tuscaninn.com • Dis. access • $$

7 Seal Rock Inn
Handy for Cliff House and Land's End *(see p115)*, as well as the Palace of the Legion of Honor. Rooms are large, though plain, and there's free parking. ✆ 545 Point Lobos Ave • Map A3 • (415) 752-8000 • www.sealrockinn.com • $$

8 Jackson Court
Located in Pacific Heights, this is a magnificent 1900 brownstone mansion. The wood-paneled parlor is an inviting place, and the stone fireplace provides a warm glow for afternoon tea. ✆ 2198 Jackson St • Map F2 • (415) 929-7670 • www.jacksoncourt.com • $$$

9 Twin Peaks Hotel
Clean, quiet and comfortable, but it doesn't get any simpler than this. The advantage is the close proximity to the Castro, Hayes Valley, and the Mission. ✆ 2160 Market St • Map F4 • (415) 863-2909 • Some en-suite bathrooms • No air conditioning • $

10 Pacific Heights Inn
On a quiet block close to transport, this motel is modern and comfortable. Free on-site parking, Wi-Fi, and Continental breakfast. Some rooms have kitchens. ✆ 1555 Union St • Map F2 • (415) 776-3310 • www.pacificheightsinn.com • No air conditioning • $

Note: Unless otherwise stated, all hotels accept credit cards, and have en suite bathrooms and air conditioning

Price Categories

For a standard, double room per night (with breakfast if included), taxes and extra charges.

$	under $100
$$	$100–$200
$$$	$200–$250
$$$$	$250–$300
$$$$$	over $300

Above **Inn on Castro**

🔟 Gay and Lesbian Hotels

1 Inn on Castro
The very friendly owner of this B&B seems to have thought of everything to make your stay in the heart of the Castro as pleasurable as possible. He's ready with maps and advice on where to go. Comfort is key, in bright rooms filled with art and plants. ✆ *321 Castro St • Map E5 • (415) 861-0321 • www.innon castro.com • No air conditioning • Dis. access • $$*

2 Chateau Tivoli
Rooms and suites in this stunning old building are named after Mark Twain, Enrico Caruso, Jack London, and others, to remind guests of San Francisco's illustrious history in the arts. Rooms are furnished with four-poster beds, fireplaces, and bay windows. ✆ *1057 Steiner St • Map E3 • (415) 776-5462 • www.chateautivoli.com • No air conditioning • $$*

3 The Willows Inn
This restored 1903 Edwardian house is conveniently located close to public transport in Castro's gay community. The interior is a blend of handcrafted willow furnishings, antique dressers, and cozy comforters. Kimono bathrobes are also provided. ✆ *710 14th St • Map E4 • (415) 431-4770 • www.willowssf.com • No en suite bathrooms • No air conditioning • $$*

4 24 Henry Village Guesthouse
This charming building was constructed in the Victorian style in the late 1880s. It is situated on a quiet, tree-lined street just three blocks from the Castro. All of the six rooms have high ceilings and period furniture. Guests can enjoy free wireless Internet connection and a complimentary breakfast. ✆ *24 Henry St • Map F4 • (415) 864-5686, (800) 900-5684 • www.24henry.com • No air conditioning • $*

5 Castro Suites
This restored 1890s Italianate Victorian has views of Downtown and the Bay. With a minimum 30-day stay, accommodations are a mixture of contemporary furniture, original art, and plants. The kitchen is equipped with dishwasher, clothes washer, and microwave. ✆ *927 14th St • Map E4 • (415) 437-1783 • www.castrosuites.com • No air conditioning • Dis. access • $$$*

6 Renoir Hotel
A friendly, gay boutique hotel with the best views of the gay pride march on Market St. Built in 1909, its European turn-of-the-century charm has since been restored. Check out their great online rates before booking. ✆ *45 McAllister St • Map Q3 • (415) 626-5200 • www.renoirhotel.com • No air conditioning • $$*

7 The Inn San Francisco
This fine Victorian mansion serves a buffet breakfast in charming parlors. The garden has a redwood hot tub, and sundeck with a panoramic view of the city. ✆ *943 South Van Ness St • Map F5 • (415) 641-0188 • www.innsf.com • No air conditioning • $$*

8 The Parker Guest House
This Edwardian mini-mansion has expansive gardens and sun decks. Just steps away from gay bars and restaurants. ✆ *520 Church St • Map F5 • (415) 621-3222 • www.parkerguesthouse.com • No air conditioning • $$*

9 Bel Abri
Rooms feature shutters, French tapestries, and wrought-iron pieces. Most rooms include a fireplace, and two of the rooms also have Jacuzzis. ✆ *837 California Blvd, Napa • (877) 561-6000 • www.belabri.net • Dis. access • $$*

10 Meadowlark Country House
In the heart of the Wine Country, this elegant guesthouse is situated on an estate with great facilities such as a mineral pool, hot tub, sauna, and whirlpool spa. ✆ *601 Petrified Forest Rd, Calistoga • (707) 942-5651 • www.meadowlarkinn.com • No air conditioning • $$*

San Francisco is, of course, a tolerant city and virtually all hotels will welcome gay and lesbian guests with a smile.

Left **The Mosser** Right **San Remo**

🔟 Budget Hotels and Hostels

1 Coventry Motor Inn

A good, basic motel, offering large pleasant rooms with bay windows, located on the Marina's "Motel Row." It isn't beautiful, but it's functional and reliable. All rooms are no-smoking, and parking is complimentary. A minimum stay may apply on some weekends. 🕲 *1901 Lombard St • Map F2 • (415) 567-1200 • www.coventrymotorinn. com • Dis. access • $*

2 Good Hotel

The Good Hotel promises a stylish, sustainable stay at a great price. Even though the rooms are on the small side, they have iPod docking stations, free Wi-Fi, and the decor is modern and clean. Bicycles are also available for guest use. 🕲 *112 7th St • Map R3 • (415) 621-7001 • www. thegoodhotel.com • No air conditioning • $*

3 The Mosser

It's hard to beat this location, less than a block from the center of Market Street and the nearest subway station. The Mosser has a few other things going for it as well, namely clean, Ikea-furnished rooms, great prices, and a terrific bistro off its lobby. 🕲 *54 4th St • Map Q4 • (415) 986-4400 • www. themosser.com • No air conditioning • $*

4 Cow Hollow Motor Inn and Suites

Larger-than-average rooms. Floral wallpaper and traditional furniture give it a homey feel. Some suites have Oriental carpets accenting wood floors, marble fireplaces, and antiques. Free parking, a no-smoking hotel. 🕲 *2190 Lombard St • Map E2 • (415) 921-5800 • www.cowhollowmotorinn. com • Dis. access • $*

5 Marina Inn

The charm of a San Francisco Victorian awaits you here. The marble lobby is the focal point of this four-story hotel built in 1924, and the sitting room is the setting for Continental breakfasts. But the real draw is the price and the location, which can't be beat. 🕲 *3110 Octavia St at Lombard • Map F2 • (415) 928-1000 • www.marinainn. com • No air conditioning • Dis. access • $*

6 San Remo

North Beach's biggest bargain is full of charms. Each room is decorated with antiques, and the corridors feature brass railings and hanging plants under skylights. Every room has its own sink, while other facilities are down the hall. 🕲 *2237 Mason St • Map K3 • (415) 776-8688 • www.sanremohotel.com • No en suite bathrooms • No air conditioning • $*

7 Hostelling International Downtown

Action-central for all the major sights. Rooms hold up to five beds. All major public transportation is just outside and there's lots of tourist info too. 🕲 *312 Mason St • Map P3 • (415) 788-5604 • www. norcalhostels.org • No en suite bathrooms • No air conditioning • $*

8 Hostelling International Fisherman's Wharf

This hostel offers free breakfast, Wi-Fi, and parking. It's just a short walk to everything along the Bayshore. 🕲 *Fort Mason, Bldg. 240 • Map F1 • (415) 771-7277 • www. norcalhostels.org • Dis. access • $*

9 San Francisco Zen Center

The center has several comfortable, quiet rooms available for those who are interested in learning about Zen practices. 🕲 *300 Page St • Map F4 • (415) 863-3136 • www. sfzc.org • Dis. access • No en suite bathrooms • No air conditioning • $*

10 Marin Headlands Hostel

Nearby are the Muir Woods, and great beaches. 🕲 *Fort Barry, Bldg 941, Field & Bunker Rds • (415) 331-2777 • www.norcalhostels.org • No en suite bathrooms • No air conditioning • $*

Price Categories

For a standard, double room per night (with breakfast if included), taxes and extra charges.

$	under $100
$$	$100–$200
$$$	$200–$250
$$$$	$250–$300
$$$$$	over $300

Above **The Gateway**

TOP 10 Apartments and Private Homes

1 Oakwood Pine Street

With a minimum stay of 30 days and starting prices lower than most hotels, these apartments offer one- and two-bedroom options, all with private balconies and fully equipped kitchens. Many have views of the Bay Bridge and the Financial District. A great location, too. ✆ *1 Pine St at Market • Map N6 • (877) 902-0832 • No air conditioning • www. oakwood.com • $$$*

2 The Gateway

Location is everything at these fully furnished, extended-stay apartments, which are just steps away from a host of retail stores, restaurants, and local transportation options. Offering every amenity and service one could possibly want when planning a long visit, these apartments promise a convenient and comfortable stay. ✆ *460 Davis Court • Map N6 • (888) 220-0301 • www.execustay. com • Dis. access • $$*

3 Pinnacle Suites

An all-suite hotel on Nob Hill. The rooms offer kitchens with refrigerators and microwaves. There are housekeeping and laundry services, voice mail, cable TV, and a valet service (small fee). ✆ *899 Pine St • Map N3 • (415) 421-1899 • www. thepinnacleatnobhill.com • Dis. access • $$*

4 VRBO

The VRBO or Vacation Rentals By Owner website is used by many people in this area. Private homes, condos, and townhouses include the types of properties listed on the site as well as the dates they are available to hire. It is a wonderful alternative to staying in hotels, especially for travelers in larger groups or families. • *www.vrbo.com*

5 Casa Luna

This restored Edwardian building has been converted into two luxury apartments in the heart of the Castro district. It boasts eco-friendly, stylish furnishings, Egyptian cotton sheets, and Jacuzzi soaking tubs. Each apartment has two bedrooms and two full baths and is in a very safe and convenient location. ✆ *4058 17th St between Market & Castro • Map E5 • (415) 738-8121 • www.casalunasf.com • No air conditioning • Dis. access • $$$$*

6 Air BnB

This popular apartment accommodation website is being called the "Ebay for space". A wide range of places to stay is on offer, from rooms in apartments to whole houses. ✆ *(415) 800-5959 • www.airbnb. com • $–$$$, depending on facilities and placement*

7 The Monroe Hotel

Amid the mansions of Pacific Heights, the Monroe combines the best of a hotel and an apartment. American-style breakfasts and four-course dinners are included. Maid service is also provided. ✆ *1870 Sacramento St • Map N1 • (415) 474-6200 • www. monroeresidenceclub.com • No air conditioning • Dis. access • $*

8 Bed & Breakfast San Francisco

All homes participating in the service have been carefully selected. Private residences in every desirable part of San Francisco are listed, including Pacific Heights and the Marina, as well as farther afield in Marin County and the Wine country. ✆ *1-800-452-8249 or (415) 899-0060 • www. bbsf.com • $–$$, depending on placement*

9 Home Exchange Inc.

Home exchangers simply trade their homes at a time that is convenient to both parties. ✆ *1-800-877-8723 or (310) 798-3864 • www.homeexchange.com*

10 The Invented City

This home exchange agency provides web access to members worldwide who exchange their homes for short- and long-term stays. ✆ *41 Sutter St • www. invented-city.com*

General Index

Acknowledgments

Main Contributors
Native San Franciscan Jeffrey Kennedy now lives mainly in Italy and Spain. A graduate of Stanford University, he spends his time producing, writing and acting. He is also co-author of *Top 10 Rome* and author of *Top 10 Mallorca* and *Top 10 Miami & The Keys*.

Produced by Sargasso Media Ltd, London

Editorial Director Zoë Ross
Art Editor Janis Utton
Picture Research Helen Stallion
Proofreader Stewart J Wild
Indexer Hilary Bird
Editorial Assistance Tracy Becker
Main Photographer Robert Vente
Additional Photography
Trevor Hill, Neil Lukas, Andrew McKinney, Rough Guides/Angus Oborn, Dan Rubin
Illustrator chrisorr.com
Fact Checkers Dan Rubin, AnneLise Sorensen

For Dorling Kindersley
Publishing Managers
Ian Midson, Scarlett O'Hara
Publisher Douglas Amrine
Revisions Coordinators
Rose Hudson, Mani Ramaswamy, Ros Walford, Hugo Wilkinson
Assistant Revisions Coordinators
Mary Ormandy, Pollyanna Poulter
Senior Cartographic Editor
Casper Morris
DTP Jason Little
Production Melanie Dowland
Picture Librarian David Saldanha
Revisions Team
Emma Anacootee, Marta Bescos, Sherry Collins, Karen Constanti, Lisa Cope, Imogen Corke, Conrad Van Dyk, Nicola Erdpresser, Camilla Gersh, Lydia Halliday, Claire Jones, Bharti Karakoti, Priya Kukadia, Jude Ledger, Carly Madden, Nicola Malone, Alison McGill, Sam Merrell, Vikki Nousiainen, Catherine Palmi, Helen Partington, Susie Peachy, Andrea Pinnington, Pete Quinlan, Roseen Teare, Karen Villabona, Amy Westervelt

Maps DK India: Managing Editor Aruna Ghose; Senior Cartographer Uma Bhattacharya; Cartographic Researcher Suresh Kumar.

Special Assistance
The author would like to thank the following people for their assistance: Patricia Perez-Arce and Ed, Sonal Bhatt, Bruce and Celeste Joki, Margaret Casey and Mark Trahan, Robert Vente, Angela Jackson, Sandy Barnes, Harriet and Rick Lehrbaum, Paul Brown, Phyllis Butler, Nini Dibble, Jolie Chain, Helen Craddick, Vivian Deuschl, Marr Goodrum, and Isabelle Lejano.

Picture Credits
Key: a-above; b-below/bottom; c-centre; f-far; l-left; r-right; t-top.

The publishers would like to thank the following individuals, companies and picture libraries for their kind permission to reproduce their photographs:

21ST AMENDMENT BREWERY: 112tl.111 MINNA GALLERY: Daniel Kokin 111tl. ABSINTHE BRASSERIE & BAR: 105tl; ALAMY IMAGES: Jim Gold-stein 40tl; AMERICANO BAR: 66tr. BANCROFT LIBRARY, BERKELEY UNIVERSITY: 36tr; BIMBO'S 365 CLUB: 71tl; BLUE BOTTLE COFFEE: Clay McLachlan/ClayPix.

com 64bl; BRIAN BIGGS: 120tr. CABLE CAR MUSEUM: 11b; CALIFORNIA ACADEMY OF SCIENCES: 22b; Dong Lin 22tl, 22tr, 23br, 23tr; CAMPTON PLACE HOTEL: 114tl; CITY ART GALLERY: 110tr; THE CLIFT HOTEL: Ian Schrager Hotels, Nikolas Koerno: 114tr; CORBIS: 1, 8cl, 9, 10b, 12–13, 14–15, 16tl, 16b, 17c, 17b, 27c, 34t, 36tl, 37tr, 37br, 39, 40tr, 52tl, 52tr, 54tl, 54tr, 54b, 55r, 74b, 76tr, 78tl, 78tr, 79t; COST PLUS WORLD MARKET: 96tr. DE YOUNG MUSEUM: Mark Darley 21c. DREAMSTIME.COM: Canbalci 80–81,Coleong 117–8; Elf0724 130–1; Jancsikb 86–7; Rramirez125 102–3; Tinnaporn 4–5. ENCHANTED CRYSTAL: photo by David J Landry 104tl. THE FAIRMONT SAN FRANCISCO HOTEL 70tl; Courtesy of the FINE ARTS MUSEUM OF SAN FRANCISCO: 114tl; FREY NORRIS GALLERY: 42tl; THE GATEWAY: 149tl; GETTY IMAGES: FilmMagic / C Flanigan 67tl; Ronald Martinez 73r; HARVEY'S SF: 68tr; HOUSERSTOCK: Jan Butchofsky – Houser 18t; Dave G Houser 15cr, 18–19, 75tl; THE LARK CREEK INN: 129tl; LE COLONIAL: 70tl; TERRENCE MCCARTHY: 56b; SEAN MORIARTY: 74tr; THE MOSSER HOTEL: 148tl; MUSEUM OF CRAFT & FOLK ART: *Baby Frog 2001*, blown and sand-carved glass, 11 x 10¾ x 8 inches Archie Noise Cat photo Lee Fatheree 42b. Courtesy of OAKLAND MUSEUM OF CALIFORNIA: 126tc, 126tr. POLANCO GALLERY OF MEXICAN ARTS: 104tr; PRESS CLUB: 66bl, 90tl. REDFERNS: David Redfern 54tc; REX FEATURES: 37cl, 53tl; RON-ALD GRANT ARCHIVE: MGM 53tr; Paramount Pictures 16tr; Warner Brothers 53br. Collection of the SAN FRANCISCO MUSEUM OF MODERN ART: Henrik Kam 27cb; *California Artist*, 1982 © Estate of Robert Arneson/ DACS London/VAGA, New York, 2011 27t; *Michael Jackson and Bubbles*, 1988 Jeff Koons 27bl; SAN FRANCISCO ZOO: Jason Langer 114c; SPRUCE: 62tr. STANFORD SHOPPING CENTER: 128tr. SCOMA'S: 97tl. TABLESPOON: 3tr.; TUSCAN INN: 146tr; TWENTY FIVE LUSK: 112tr. ROBERT VENTE: 20b, 32c, 32b, 33t, 34tr, 35t, 61r, 72b, 74tl, 148tl, 149. YANK SING: 91tl; JERRY YULSMAN: 52b.

For jacket credits see Contents page All other images are © Dorling Kindersley. For further information see: www.dkimages.com

Special Editions of DK Travel Guides

DK Travel Guides can be purchased in bulk quantities at discounted prices for use in promotions or as premiums. We are also able to offer special editions and personalized jackets, corporate imprints, and excerpts from all of our books, tailored specifically to meet your own needs.

To find out more, please contact:

(in the US) **specialsales@dk.com**

(in the UK) **travelspecialsales @uk.dk.com**

(in Canada) DK Special Sales at **general@tourmaline.ca**

(in Australia) **business.development @pearson.com.au**

Selected Street Index